STAGES

 of

SENIOR CARE

*Your Step-by-Step Guide to Making
the Best Decisions*

PAUL AND LORI HOGAN

New York Chicago San Francisco Lisbon London Madrid Mexico City
Milan New Delhi San Juan Seoul Singapore Sydney Toronto

Library of Congress Cataloging-in-Publication Data

Hogan, Paul, 1962 –
    Stages of senior care : your step-by-step guide to making the best decisions /
by Paul Hogan and Lori Hogan.
       p.   cm.
    ISBN 978-0-07-162109-0 (alk. paper)
    1. Older people—Care—United States.   2. Aging parents—Care—United
States.   I. Hogan, Lori.   II. Title.

HV1461.H627   2009
362.610973—dc22   2009020572

*To all family caregivers, like our mothers, Catherine Hogan
and Jan Novicki, who lovingly and heroically provide care
for the seniors in their lives*

3 4 5 6 7 8 9 10 11 12 13 14 15 16 17 18 19 20 21 22 WFR/WFR 0

ISBN 978-0-07-162109-0
MHID   0-07-162109-1

Interior photographs by Robert Ervin Photography, Inc.

McGraw-Hill books are available at special quantity discounts to use as premiums and
sales promotions or for use in corporate training programs. To contact a representative,
please visit the Contact Us pages at www.mhprofessional.com.

Contents

Preface

Caring for our seniors has changed almost beyond recognition over the past generation. A few decades ago, there were really only two choices for protecting our parents and other older adults in their declining years: we cared for them ourselves at home, or they went to a nursing home. The choice was clear, but definitely agonizing as well. If parents stayed at home, the children caring for them were often stretched beyond their physical, financial, and emotional capabilities. If the nursing home was chosen, the senior often felt abandoned, and correspondingly, their children felt gnawing guilt about their parents' anguish.

Since then, options for senior care have proliferated wonderfully. That, of course, is great and welcome news. But having such a variety of choices presents challenges of its own. How do older adults and their children and others who love them decide among the available options? How do they identify the best alternative for their circumstances while keeping in mind the important considerations of health, emotions, geography, finances, and other variables?

The task can seem overwhelming. But it doesn't need to be. To help you, we decided to write this book as a guide to what families need to know in order to make the best senior care decisions. And, although this book is directed at you and your family, including the senior members, we have also designed it to be useful to professional caregivers, medical professionals, senior care specialists, bank trust officers, elder care attorneys, physicians, and others who need to know more about the expanding universe of senior care.

We've learned much about this new world of senior care and how to navigate through the care options. The business we founded fifteen years ago provided an important window into the experiences of thousands of families, each facing decisions much like yours. The cumulative lessons learned have informed our understanding of senior care and the need for this book. Our business, Home Instead Senior Care, is the world's largest network of local franchise offices that send caregivers into homes of seniors to provide nonmedical services, such as doing light housekeeping chores, preparing meals, and probably most important, offering the older adults companionship and moral support. Home Instead Senior Care has 850 offices in fifteen countries and employs 60,000 caregivers. These caregivers have experienced the challenges faced by hundreds of thousands of seniors worldwide, as well as the struggles that their families encounter when navigating decisions related to each stage of this care continuum. We work regularly with more than 100,000 outside professionals including social workers, hospital discharge planners, care facility managers, and geriatric care managers who offer a variety of services and care options for seniors.

Our family, too, has faced decisions about how to care for its aging members. Paul's eighty-nine-year-old grandmother was rapidly declining from healthy senior status to frail and elderly. But in caring for her, we learned that with some simple changes in her routine, such as proper meals and a lot of attention from family and friends, she was able to live a wonderful, fulfilling, and happy life for twelve more years.

We have seen firsthand the confusion that overwhelms families when they lack the knowledge and understanding of how to provide care to their loved ones—and the tragedy such confusion can lead to. We have witnessed the pain that families feel when they look back on missed opportunities. On the positive side, we have also seen the blessing of a well-informed and well-handled change of life in which information and communication abound.

Clearly, we bring a viewpoint to the field of senior care and a faith in our own program. We understand the importance of helping seniors stay for as long as possible in their own homes and in the company of family. But we also recognize that there are many cases in which seniors will be happier and healthier in alternative programs. Some, for example, will be more comfortable in the company of peers in an assisted living community. Seniors with serious disabling illnesses requiring extensive, around-the-clock medical attention may be far better off in high-quality nursing homes.

In this book we seek to present, fully and fairly, the options open to you and your family, including the advantages and drawbacks of each and the financial consequences. We recognize that one of your goals will be not only to take care of an aging member of your family but to hold your family together and preserve your own well-being by involving siblings and others in this undertaking. You can feel assured that by the conclusion of this book, you will have done your best to research your alternatives in order to navigate through a challenging, but potentially very rewarding, time of life.

Our wish is that you will use this information to provide the best and most appropriate senior care for those you love and that, as a result, you and your family will have the satisfaction of knowing you did your best for those you love the most.

Acknowledgments

The authors gratefully acknowledge the extraordinarily diligent efforts of the following individuals who made this book possible: Jim Beck, who initiated and managed the project from start to finish; The Dilenschneider Group, with special appreciation to Bob Dilenschneider and Joe Tessitore, who proposed this book to McGraw-Hill Publishing and then worked with us to make it a reality; Lee Smith, who helped prepare and revise the original manuscript; Larry Novicki, who edited the draft manuscript; Brian Mainwaring, who organized and directed the research team that provided the material for this book; the team itself, which included Georgene Lahm, Kathy Rygg, Sherry Thompson, and Judith Sexton; a legal team made up of Jisella Dolan, Cindy Wooden, Pete Salsich III, and Jeff Jarecki, who advised on copyright issues, obtained permissions, and handled myriad other project-related legal tasks; Bill Comfort, C.S.A., C.L.T.C., who reviewed some of the book's most complicated material; and Dan Wieberg, who led the efforts to market and publicize this work.

In addition, our thanks go to the many individuals who shared with us stories about their relationships with senior family members and friends, stories that appear throughout the book that we hope will help to personalize the narrative for you. As you'll see, these are families that, over the years, found themselves searching for just the types of senior care options detailed in this book. We realize that for many of these sources, their recollections were very pleasant, but for others, revisiting these memories may have proven difficult and painful. All of you who volunteered to tell your personal stories know who you are; please know how much we appreciate your having done so.

And, finally, we wish to extend our appreciation to the family of Home Instead Senior Care franchise owners whose support and contributions made them "coauthors" of this book.

A Whole New World

The realization comes unexpectedly and suddenly; or it's a gradual awakening that can no longer be ignored. Yesterday you were your mother's daughter, or your father's daughter, as you have been all your life, through all of life's passages— but the passages were always yours. You were the one who was a disruptive three-year-old, compliant ten-year-old, rebellious adolescent, overconfident college student, confused novice in the workplace, cocky associate director, nervous newlywed, and then a sometimes-overwhelmed parent of your own three-year-old.

Through it all, your mother never changed. She was the rock, home base. Your tumultuous spinning from stage to stage may have exasperated her from time to time, but she rarely showed it. She was the fixed point in your small universe, the one you could always rely on to get you out of that impossible jam, that catastrophic situation, or so it seemed at the time.

That Was Yesterday

Today is very different. This morning you drove to your mother's house for a routine visit and found her sitting in her car in the driveway, making no effort to move the car or get out. When you asked her to roll down the window, she did, and she recognized you. But she had no idea where she was or where she was going.

The episode confirms a truth you had been trying to hide from—your mother's growing detachment from the world around her. On your last several visits, her home has been in disarray, extraordinary neglect on the part of a woman who had been a diligent housekeeper to the point of obsession all your life.

Or perhaps the realization that your parents are no longer your protectors but now your dependents comes with your father's spinal injury. He was always Mr. Fix-It—electrician, carpenter, plumber, roofer all in one. Not only did he take care of your parents' home, he was the one you called when your furnace collapsed in midwinter, your own husband far less adept with tools. Now your father is likely to be a semi-invalid for the rest of his life, confined to a wheelchair much of the time.

Who Takes Responsibility?

The world is now turned upside down. You have suddenly become your parents' parent. And you realize that the coming years are going to be extremely challenging. How do you talk to your parents about their changed lives and bring them in on the decision about what kind of care they need? How do you engage your siblings in sharing the responsibilities? Which sibling should be the health care proxy, and should he have absolute authority?

Who should manage the finances and protect your parents' assets? How do you distinguish between a good assisted living center and a bad one before your parent is already in residence? How do you know which option of the senior care continuum best suits you parents' needs now? What information do you need to make the best decisions about care options? We will address these and many other important issues throughout this book to help you make wise and responsible senior care decisions.

You are understandably devastated by the realization that your mother or father is failing. The fear had crossed your mind from time to time in recent years after they reached the age of seventy, but you pushed your concern aside in favor of more immediate worries, like college tuitions for your children. You are likely feeling guilty because you hadn't been more insistent that your parents buy long-term care insurance and create advance directives. You are afraid that the decisions you make in the coming months are going to shorten your mother's life, or worse, make her final years miserable.

You Are Not Alone

Also, you may feel angry—angry, in large part, because you feel that you are alone, that you must manage your mother's or your father's care by yourself, perhaps with only grudging assistance from your siblings.

Fortunately, that is not true. You are not alone. The enterprise of caring for the elderly has grown prodigiously in the past few years. Which isn't surprising. The senior population in the United States is increasing at an astonishing rate. Some 38.7 million Americans are now sixty-five or older.[1] That population is expected to more than double in the first half of this century, from 35 million in 2000[2] to 88.5 million in 2050.[3] (See Figure 1.1.) The fastest growing part of the U.S. population is the very old, that is, those over eighty-five. That group is projected to double from 4.6 million in 2002 to 9.6 million in 2030[4]—and double again to 20.9 million in 2050.[5] (See Figure 1.2.)

Moreover, it is not just the United States that is experiencing this huge growth in its elderly population. Aging is truly a global

Figure 1.1   U.S. SENIOR POPULATION AGE 65+

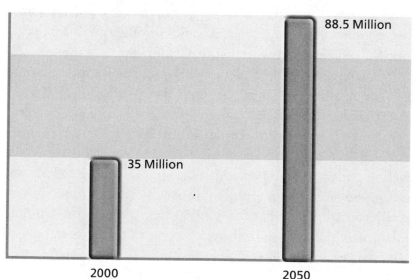

88.5 Million

35 Million

2000   2050

phenomenon. The population of the United Kingdom over eighty years old has increased by more than 1.1 million between 1981 and 2007.[6] People seventy-five and older now constitute 10 percent of the population of Japan.[7] In 2007, people sixty-five and older made up 13 percent of Australia's population; by 2056 those over sixty-five are expected to constitute 23 percent or more of the population.[8] In many developing countries, especially those of Asia and Latin America, the elderly population is expected to grow by as much as 300 percent by 2025.[9]

An Expanding World of Care Choices

Fortunately, however, a flourishing senior care industry is prepared to help take care of them. In the United States alone, the size of the home care market in 2007 was more than $57.6 billion.[10] There are currently about 16,000 certified nursing homes with some 1.4 million residents.[11] Also, according to the National Center for Assisted Living, an additional 1 million seniors live in

Figure 1.2   U.S. SENIOR POPULATION AGE 85+

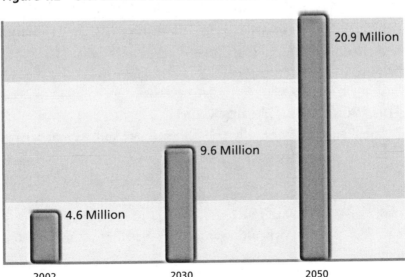

20.9 Million	
9.6 Million	
4.6 Million	

2002   2030   2050

up to 38,000 assisted living residences, which provide some help with daily living but not around-the-clock nursing care.[12] An even larger group of Americans with long-term health problems, about 7.6 million of them, remain at home suffering from acute illness, most of it related to aging. They are supported by a cadre of 83,000 caregivers, who visit them in their homes, cook meals, do light housework, and provide companionship.[13]

Among the many others who can be called upon to help the elderly are 7,600 geriatricians (physicians specializing in the care of seniors)[14] and about 4,400 elder law attorneys.[15] Hundreds of churches and synagogues across the country now sponsor adult care centers and other programs to help the elderly.

So, you are not alone. Indeed, you have entered a heavily populated and complex new world that is changing rapidly. Professionals ranging from research scientists in their laboratories to hands-on caregivers at the bedside learn more and more about the care of the elderly and how to apply those lessons. What you must do is learn how to find your way through the maze of services that are available and how to determine which are best for you and your parent. And you need to be armed with information to avoid the misunderstandings, deceptions, conflicts of interest, and misleading information that develop in any industry—the senior care industry sadly being no exception.

The Evolution of Senior Care

Throughout history, families, both immediate and extended, have borne the primary responsibility for taking care of their elderly, just as they do today. Elder care institutions and organizations beyond the home appear to have been rare before modern times.

Still, a few advanced societies through the ages may have recognized a community responsibility for the elderly. One of those

Centenarians: Expect More, Many More

The remote corner of the federal government known as the White House Greetings Office is becoming a busy place. That's the desk from which the president sends good tidings to Americans who have reached significant milestones in their lives, including fiftieth wedding anniversaries and hundredth birthdays. The number of centenarians in the United States jumped from some 50,400 in 2000[16] to more than 84,000 by the end of 2007.[17] That's an increase of 67 percent. By the year 2040, the number of centenarians is expected to top 580,000,[18] or about the equivalent of the current population of Washington, D.C.[19]

Figure 1.3   U.S. CENTENARIANS

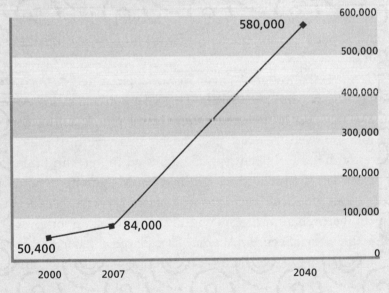

societies was the Byzantine Empire. Weak and ill older citizens were sometimes cared for in special infirmaries, called *gerocomeia*, according to several researchers at National Athens University in Greece. In the twelfth century, Emperor John II Comnenus established the most famous of the *gerocomeia* in the Constantinople monastery and hospital of the Pantocrator. In their heyday, these forerunners of the modern nursing home operated all over the empire, mostly in or near the monasteries. They were highly esteemed, and the governor of the institution seems to have been a person of real importance.[20]

The evolution of community participation in elder care was more complicated in many parts of the world and not such an honored undertaking. As an example, for several centuries in England, seniors were subject to the country's Poor Laws, which often left them with "a stark choice between destitution and the workhouse."[21] Indeed, according to the 1901 census, more than 208,000 people were residents of workhouses in England and Wales.[22]

German Chancellor Otto von Bismarck pioneered the recognition of seniors as a group worthy of special protection by instituting an old-age social insurance program in 1889.[23] Other developed nations followed. For instance, the 1935 passage in the United States of the Social Security Act addressed the pressing issue of long-term economic security for the country's seniors—a population whom President Franklin Roosevelt said previously may have "spent their remaining years within the walls of a poorhouse."[24] Thus, the Social Security Act may have played a major role in the evolution in the United States of the proprietary nursing home.

Grandmother's Few Choices

When your mother and father were faced a generation ago with the challenge of how to care for your failing grandmother, they

Rewarding Experiences

Taking care of your aging parent does not have to be a crushing, dispiriting, or impoverishing experience. Let there be no doubt, though, it will end, almost certainly, with the death of someone you love very much and with all of the accompanying grief. But before that inevitability, there can be rewarding experiences that will equal any of the other high plateaus in your previous relationship with your mother or father.

Ruth, one caregiver, told us, "Quite honestly the last eighteen months of Mother's life were wonderful. My father had been the social one, and he and Mom spent most of their time together. When Dad died, my sisters and I would take Mom for girls' afternoon outings to lunch or the movies. We'd take turns bringing meals to her home. Those days with Mom were among the best our family ever had."

This book will help you experience similar bonds and achieve insights into your relationships with your parents and siblings. This is the book of best endings. But let us be clear. This is not a medical book. It will not help you understand in detail your parent's disease or prognosis. Moreover, you will still need your Bible or other spiritual resources and religious and family counselors, other professional therapists, and mentors for guidance and comfort.

But as a practical and comprehensive guide for understanding the world of senior care and navigating through all of its challenges as your parent's needs change, this may be the most valuable book you could read.

had only a few choices: They could leave her at home and set up shifts with other relatives to bring her meals and help with chores. They could bring her into their own home with all of the disruption that move would entail, weighed against your parents' satisfaction in knowing they were demonstrating their great love for her. Or, they could send her to a nursing home, where the care would be professional, but she would feel at sea, perhaps abandoned.

In the years since your parents had to make that fateful decision for their own parents, the field of senior care has matured far beyond what your parents would have recognized as alternatives.

Taking Advantage of the Advances in Care

Science's knowledge of what actually happens to our bodies and minds as we pass into old age has grown exponentially, producing therapies undreamed of years ago and dispelling many of the

Elder Gender

Throughout the book we refer informally and interchangeably to your loved one as "Mom" or "Dad," "him" or "her." We use the female form more often than the male, however, and that is deliberate. Women live longer than men. Indeed, over the age of eighty-five, women outnumber men by a ratio of 2.3 to 1.[25] Typically, although not inevitably, as a married couple ages, the husband, likely a few years older than his wife, becomes frail before she does. She often cares for him with relatively little outside help until he passes away. Then she is left alone, and as she becomes frail, she needs help from outside caregivers, either family members or professionals.

myths about old age. Those advances have also allowed seniors to live longer, thereby leading to more options in care.

For example, senility (or cognitive decline), it is now understood, is not a normal part of healthy aging. There are certain changes in cognitive health that will occur as people age, such as a slower learning pace. However, cognitive decline may be prevented, or at least forestalled, by relatively simple measures, such as remaining physically active, controlling high blood pressure, and regularly engaging in social activities.[26] Alzheimer's, on the other hand, has been recognized as a specific aging-related disease, and although there is not yet a cure (or a proven means of prevention),[27] billions are being spent on its research, and the treatment of Alzheimer's patients has greatly improved.

In previous eras, the infirm were generally encouraged to go easy on themselves physically. However, we now know that physical activity can improve health and quality of life for people of all ages—including seniors. Aside from being better able to fight chronic diseases, seniors who exercise have stronger hearts, their muscles are more fit and flexible, their bones and joints strengthened, and their moods enhanced. Exercise helps decrease the need for hospitalizations, doctor visits, and even medications.[28]

Moreover, in part because of these advances, seniors have many more options than staying home alone, moving into a grown child's home, or going to a nursing home. Those choices and how to make them are in large part the subject of this book. (For a brief look at what lies ahead in this book, please see the box "Senior Choices" later in this chapter.)

Ask Questions and Be Flexible

The proliferation of choices is a wonderful boon, because it will greatly lift the quality of your loved one's life as well. The variety of choices, however, produces a weight of its own. There is no single option that is right for all families at all times. Indeed, there is likely no single option that will be right for any family throughout the course of any senior's aging.

The family has to be much more flexible than it was in the era when the choice was binary—home or nursing home. The family has to ask more questions, separate superficial differences from real ones, and be prepared to modify or even reverse decisions already acted upon if circumstances change or if a choice isn't working out as hoped.

Adapt the Home (and Keep Adapting Your Care Plan)

Generally, there is a continuum of care that begins with the elderly family member staying at home with some modifications of the surroundings, such as grab bars in the bathtub and the replacement of doorknobs with easy-to-grip handles. Your mother may be well cared for in her own home with visiting professional help for a long time before finally moving to a nursing home or assisted living facility. Conversely, she might spend time in a nursing home because of a broken hip, say, but recuperate sufficiently to return to an assisted care facility or her own home.

How do you, she, and other members of the family make those choices? A wrong decision, or the right decision delayed, can have terrible consequences. The number of variables can be bewildering. Obviously, the senior's wishes are a priority consideration—and overwhelmingly, seniors say they want to stay at home until the ends of their lives. In fact, a recent AARP study indicated that 89 percent of Americans aged fifty or older want to age in place—that is, remain in their own homes as long as possible.[29]

However, many seniors also express concern about being a burden to their children or grandchildren. In fact, for many older adults—whose residences represent their single biggest assets—

one of the most common plans is to leave their homes to future generations, thus providing adult children and grandchildren with a substantial financial legacy.[30]

Pick the Right Experts

Our goal with this book is to help answer these questions—and many others—that you will surely face as you guide your parents through the closing years of their lives:

- How do you choose the advisors who will help you decide whether it's possible to keep your mother at home?
- How much medical care will she need and where?
- Where do you find an elder law attorney who will help you understand matters like health care proxies and living wills, procedures for using your mother's assets to pay for her care, and taxes?
- What kind of care can your mother, and you, afford?
- What long-term care insurance, if any, does she have, and will it cover in-home care as well as nursing home care?
- How does the government help?
- What are the warning signs that an organization or institution you are dealing with is directing you in a manner that is more in its own self-interest than in your mother's best interest?

And, of course, as you, your mother, and the rest of your family go through the process of settling your mother into the right support system, you will begin to think of your own future. The odds are high that your mother's current situation will someday be yours. What should you be doing now to prepare yourself for that likelihood? This subject will be discussed in detail in Chapter 19.

Senior Choices

Lifestyle alternatives are far more extensive these days. Each of the following will be explained in detail in later chapters.

- **Aging in place.** The senior remains at home. Living quarters are made friendlier and safer with the addition of such aids as hand railings in the bathtub. Sometimes seniors in the same neighborhood create an informal "village" to contract for commonly needed services like transportation and plumbing.
- **Family care.** The family bears the entire responsibility for taking care of the elderly person—either in the senior's home or in the home of a family member.
- **Senior centers.** Seniors may drop in at these gathering places for social engagement and nutritional, inexpensive meals. These are generally for seniors who can drive or walk to the centers.
- **Adult care centers.** The senior continues to live at home but spends much of the day with peers at a local community center.
- **Nonmedical care at home.** Professional caregivers come to the senior's home (and often other care settings) to provide companionship and home helper services such as meal preparation and light housework.
- **Medical care at home.** The senior may need professional medical help for easing respiratory problems, intravenous feeding, or assistance with medications—services not provided by nonmedical organizations.
- **Independent living communities.** These are also referred to as retirement communities. Seniors live in apartments or houses, generally smaller and easier to care for than

the homes they have previously lived in. Shops and movie theaters are close by, which minimizes the need for a car.

- **Assisted living centers.** Seniors here live in their own apartments, but in the same buildings or cluster of buildings. They take at least some of their meals in a common dining room but otherwise live independently. Medical help is generally close by.
- **Skilled nursing homes.** These were once thought of as institutions where the elderly were simply warehoused until they died. Now the best nursing homes include both mental and physical therapy as well as musical, art, and similar activities to help seniors extend their active lives.
- **Palliative care and hospice.** This is end-of-life treatment. A hospice can be a separate institution or part of a hospital. Or it can also be simply a form of care in other physical surroundings, including the home. The senior is made comfortable, fed, and given water and painkillers. But there is no medical intervention to prolong life.

2

You, the Caregiver

I f you are a senior who has purchased this book, we applaud you—not only in appreciation of the confidence that you have placed in us but, more important, because you have had the courage to investigate a future that so many of us try to hide from, even though such evasion almost always leads to greater pain for both seniors and their families.

Probably, however, you have bought this book because you are the relative of a senior, the eldest daughter most likely, but possibly the son, niece, brother, or even neighbor. You have taken upon yourself a leading role in the care of a senior who is either in decline or you fear on the verge of decline.

Take Pride in Giving

It is an act of great responsibility and love and of great honor. Although it doesn't show up on résumés as awards or citations that have been won or earned in our careers, hobbies, or sports, there is no prouder assertion a human being can make than "I took care of my mother and father in their final years." That proud statement is one that connects us to generations of ancestors who have gone before and taken that obligation. By taking responsibility for helping your parent, or another senior, you are setting forth on a trail that has many steps, some far more difficult than others, but few of them easy.

We want to pay special tribute to those individuals who are true Samaritans, who accept the role of protector over those who are not members of their immediate families but are members of the human family.

James of Bakersfield, California, is a dedicated and compassionate retiree who has cared for his best friend, Ron, in his own home for years. James, who had earlier cared for his own wife as well as mother and two grandmothers, took Ron, a former employee and friend for twenty years, into his home after James's wife died. "I do not consider myself a hero at all when it comes to caring for Ron," James wrote in an essay. "I have an ulterior motive here. When my wife passed away, I was at a horrible loss. But Ron gave me a great opportunity to have the will to carry on. Life is good to us both."

It would be unusual indeed for a senior to proceed from a normal, unassisted routine in his or her own home directly to a nursing home, for example, without a number of intermediate steps. In some cases, seniors retrace some of their steps. Guiding a senior through these steps is gratifying, but it can also be demanding, confusing, tiring, and frustrating.

As we mentioned previously, it sometimes happens that the senior himself, or herself, decides that the time has come to make a significant change in life, giving up the car keys, for example, or hiring someone to come in and help with the housework. Recent Home Instead Senior Care research indicates that for seniors under the age of seventy-five, the decision to take charge of managing their own care needs is initiated by the senior only about 25 percent of the time. For the other 75 percent and almost all of those over the age of seventy-five, the decision begins with someone else—a neighbor, an attorney, a doctor, or a clergyman—who first notices that the senior is in need of some support. In most cases it is the senior's child who spots the change and responds to it.

The 40-70 Rule

When you see a change, we invite you to take advantage of a public education program developed by Home Instead that we call the "40-70 Rule," a guide to conversation starters for adult children and their senior loved ones. (It is available free online at 4070talk.com.) We recommend that the conversation begin even before there is a hint of a problem; let it start when either the senior reaches the age of seventy or the oldest child forty, whichever comes first.[1]

Those ages are a bit arbitrary, perhaps, but defensible. Even the exceptional seventy-year-old who has not yet felt the onset of back pain or is slower coming up with answers while watching "Jeopardy" must acknowledge that old age is within view. And a forty-year-old is solidly established in middle age, no longer a youngster whose advice can be brushed aside. The seventy-year-old and the forty-year-old are both clearheaded, secure in the present.

Noticing Changes

Nonetheless, most of us have many important, urgent issues to deal with, from children's school performance to workplace stress, so it's understandable if the start of the 40-70 conversation gets put off. Even so, the conversation should definitely begin before there is dramatic evidence of a problem. When your father is at the wheel, you recognize that he no longer picks up on clues like the illuminated brake lights on the car in front of him as quickly as he used to. That would be a good occasion to begin a calm, two-way discussion about whether he should limit his driving, avoid the heavy traffic of rush hour, perhaps, or cut out night driving, with its murky visibility. Listen carefully to what he has to say about your suggestions.[2]

The senior might not be the first to discern his need, for a couple of understandable reasons. First, the change has been so gradual that from his perspective it is not detectable. Yes, he tailgates. But he's done so all his life and can boast that in sixty years of driving he's never had an accident. What he hasn't factored into it is that his reaction time has slowed considerably so that he can no longer hit the brakes and avoid collisions with the same assurance he once did.

Or, you might notice more subtle changes. Mom has always been so proud of her housekeeping that she is certain that she still sets the community standard for cleanliness. If she lets dirty clothes pile up to the point that the smell is offensive (to you), well, that's the way it's supposed to be. Or so she sees it.

But you've noticed the changes. You won't let your kids ride in the car when Dad is driving anymore. You wash Mom's clothes yourself when you visit. But those are just stopgap measures. Keeping your kids out of Dad's car doesn't protect other kids crossing the street, and it certainly doesn't safeguard Dad. If Mom is forgetting to wash her clothes, she's probably forgetting other things as well.

How to Respond

Now what? Except in extreme cases, as when there is severe physical incapacity, advanced dementia, or Alzheimer's, it can be a terrible injustice to force a change of life upon an unwilling senior. A colleague recalls an experience in Japan some years ago. An executive of a European airline assigned to Tokyo for several years brought along not only his wife and daughters but his reluctant seventy-five-year-old mother-in-law as well. She spoke no Japanese or English, a second language in Japan, and was therefore isolated and miserable, the victim of a well-meaning family convinced they knew what was best for her.

How do you convince your father that he needs help? Start with a reality check. Are you the only one who has noticed that Dad's driving is in decline, or has your sister or his golf partner noticed it as well? Don't assemble a family conference on the subject just yet, because you might accidentally ignite a crowd panic of sorts that invents other symptoms where there are none. So talk individually and calmly to those who know Dad. Do they notice any change in his driving? If they don't, probably you should let the matter rest for a time. Because if Dad doesn't notice a change and the others closest to him don't notice a change, your chances of convincing him are almost nil, no matter how right you are.[3]

Let's assume that others agree with you that Dad has a driving problem or Mom a housekeeping problem. How do you approach him or her? In devising the 40-70 Rule discussed earlier, we at Home Instead Senior Care conducted extensive telephone interviews with 1,000 people between forty-five and sixty-two years of age on the difficult and touchy subject of giving direction to their parents, roughly in age from early seventies to mid-nineties. A surprising 31 percent of those interviewed admitted that they have trouble getting past the child-parent relationship of their formative years to talk frankly with their parents about the challenges of aging.

Raise the Issue Early and Judiciously

If you hold your anxiety inside and wait until Dad gets into a fender bender before making your point, the reactions and counterreactions are likely to get nasty. You may be tempted to shout that he's an incompetent old fool, partly in frustration with yourself for not bringing up the matter of his driving earlier. And he's going to travel back thirty years in time to when he was correcting your inept, neophyte driving. Nothing good will come of this conversation.

So bring up the issue early. When you do so, however, recognize that there are at least a couple of serious considerations in play. His ego is at stake. He is being forced to acknowledge that he is losing a capability, a freedom, a source of power—even of showmanship if he fancies expensive, exotic cars. There is also the practical consideration. In most of the United States, a car is essential at least some of the time. All true, Dad, but how do you stack that up against the chance of hitting a child, a blow from which you would never recover?

There are certainly occasions on which Dad can catch a ride with someone else with only moderate inconvenience. And when he's going to a restaurant for dinner, why not call a taxi?

That way he can comfortably have a glass or two of Chardonnay as well. Tell him to take the wine and cab money out of your inheritance. Should his driving continue to decline so that day-time driving is dangerous as well and cabs are not a good option, agencies such as Home Instead Senior Care or other local services offer incidental transportation. (See Chapter 7 for detailed information on nonmedical care at home.) Losing the car keys doesn't have to mean the loss of independence.[4]

Is It Hard Talking to Your Parents?

In a 2007 survey, these topics were cited by adult children as most difficult to speak to parents about:

- 42%   Needing to leave home
- 30%   Losing driving privileges
- 11%   Money/finances
- 11%   Health
- 5%   None

These were mentioned as the biggest obstacles to communicating difficult issues with parents:

- 31%   Continuation of parent/child role
- 16%   Parents refuse to talk
- 12%   Physical issues
- 10%   Child feels unprepared
- 8%   Distance
- 5%   Fear

Survey Methodology: 1,000 telephone interviews were completed in the United States, and 500 interviews were completed in Canada, excluding Quebec. Data analysis was performed by the Boomer Project of Richmond, VA: boomerproject.com.

Perhaps you notice that your seventy-seven-year-old mother's home is in disarray when you visit. It's possible that this is an early sign of dementia. We'll deal with the subject of dementia, including Alzheimer's, later, but for now let's assume that she has simply lost the physical strength and energy to clean a big house. You don't have to engage her in a confrontational discussion of what a shame it is that the house doesn't look the way it used to. Simply tell her that you'd like to give her a present of a helper once a week. Sometimes there is a strong case for doing nothing at all. If your eighty-five-year-old mother really wants to wear her favorite formal dress to her birthday party, even though it is obviously stained, let her do it.[5]

Making the Decisions

The transition can be gradual and subtle, but over time it often becomes clear that your parents are no longer fully capable of taking care of themselves. You step forward and offer to be the lead caregiver, or at least one of the family members driving the decisions about how care is provided for your parent. That's fine. Experience with many families in this situation demonstrates that the outcome is best if one family member, generally the oldest daughter or the daughter nearest home, takes the lead. An awkward alternative would be a full family meeting on day-to-day issues. But you are the main decision maker, remember, the leader, not the autocrat. On major policy issues, such as whether it's time for Mom to move from assisted living into a nursing home, draw all of your siblings and other relatives into the decision as best you can. Why? For one thing, you might be wrong. They might have a better idea.

But even if you are right, the process of watching a parent move through the final stages of life is an extraordinary strain on

When an Autocrat Rules

Kim had a remarkably satisfying and productive military career in Taiwan. When he retired, he went into a second successful career at a shipping company. Kim deserved a happy life in retirement. Instead, after undergoing heart surgery, he was confined to a nursing home against his will and out of proportion with his relatively minor health care needs. His son made all decisions without consulting Kim or other family members. The son picked the nursing home that was near him yet far from Kim's other family and friends. The son rarely visited. Kim became deeply depressed and wanted to escape his fourth floor prison. But he had little choice. His son had sold his home. Kim should have developed a care plan before retirement that protected his rights and wishes.

families. Decisions regarding their care can have huge financial consequences as well as emotional ones. Make your best effort to bring everyone in the family into agreement. That's not always possible, but decisions that are perceived to be autocratic can break families apart. That would be the cruelest departure of all for your mother or father. What parents want most at the end is to leave behind a happy, intact family.

In the next chapter, we will talk about the resources and procedures you need to take care of yourself and to make the best informed decisions.

Advice for Caregivers

Since no organization has more experience with the elder population—individuals age fifty and older—than the 40-million-member AARP, we asked AARP president Jennie Chin Hansen, a nurse, to give us her thoughts on caregiving. Her response follows.

- **Prepare intellectually.** Make sure you have information that will help you be as capable a caregiver as possible. There are many resources available, including websites and books.
- **Consider the emotions.** There is an emotional side to caregiving. Often you begin to change roles with the person who might have cared for you at one time. Once the child, the cared-for, now the carer. That can be a big shift.
- **The physical aspect.** Then there's the physical side. Bookmark space to take care of yourself. This *is* a necessity. We often do and do and then don't recognize we are exhausted and, thus, more prone to our own illness.
- **It's a journey.** While caregiving can be a new life journey and an important discovery, it can also be frustrating. You may need to connect and share with other people in similar circumstances, either in person or on social networking websites for caregivers. You have to understand how you feel or think. You should not feel guilty when you get angry, because these things are part of the normal course.
- **Some should not.** It may be that some people shouldn't be caregivers if, for example, they've had a rough earlier relationship with the person who needs care. You have to know what is best for you and the individual. It may

be safer emotionally, physically, and economically not to become the caregiver so that you don't find that you have done something unintentionally you'll regret later.

- **Incredible positives.** Finally, there are incredible potential positives about caregiving. It may be an opportunity to get to a new place in your relationship together and see that person and yourself in a way that you will always treasure as part of the life cycle of our humanity.

In the end, what matters most is that you are kind to yourself and your elder in this vital life stage. Caring is not just a function, it's a state of being, whether we are young or old.

If Talks Fail . . .

We recognize that throughout this chapter we assume that the senior can have calm, rational discussions about the future with his or her children. Happily, that is generally the case, especially when the conversations begin when the senior is still in reasonably good physical and mental condition. But there are cases in which for various reasons rational discussion is not possible. Please see Chapter 16 for help with those situations.

Tips: How Adult Children Should Talk to Parents

Communication expert Jake Harwood, Ph.D., from the University of Arizona, has these tips for family when talking to seniors about sensitive subjects:

- **Get started.** If you're forty or your parents are seventy, it's time to start observing and gathering information thoughtfully and carefully. Don't reach a conclusion from a single observation.   *(continued)*

- **Talk it out.** Approach your parents with a conversation. Discuss what you've observed, using concrete examples if necessary, and ask your parents what they think is going on. If your parents acknowledge the situation, ask what they think would be a good solution.
- **Sooner is best.** Talk sooner rather than later, before a crisis has occurred. If you know your loved one has poor eyesight or has trouble driving at night, begin to address those issues before a problem arises.
- **Forget the baby talk.** Remember that you are talking to an adult, not a child. Patronizing speech or baby talk will put older adults on the defensive and conveys a lack of respect.
- **Emphasize solutions that maximize independence.** Always try to move toward solutions that provide the maximum amount of independence for the older person. Look for answers that optimize strengths and compensate for problems. For instance, if your loved ones need help at home, look for tools that can help them maintain their strength.
- **Let them know that you are aware of the whole situation.** If your dad dies and your mom's house soon sinks into disarray, it's probably not because she's ill. She's lost a lifelong relationship and needs social support. Help her find it.[6]

Tips: How Parents Should Talk to Adult Children
- **Be assertive . . .** You may be patronized, put down, or abused, even by family members. Assertiveness involves figuring out what you need in a specific situation and stating that clearly so that the other person can't fail to understand.

- **. . . but not aggressive.** Negative, personal attacks on the other person may make you feel good temporarily, but they will probably enforce the other person's negative perception of you.
- **Be selective.** Save your assertive behavior for situations in which it is most important. In some circumstances, it may be easier to walk away or go along.
- **Optimize your energy.** Look for places and times in which you are most effective in getting what you need out of conversations. If you are more on your toes in the morning, arrange to meet then.
- **Recognize possible barriers.** If you have trouble hearing, get a hearing aid. If you are forgetful, make lists.
- **Avoid sounding overly dependent.** Seek social contact with people who encourage you to do things for yourself. Avoid spending lots of time in situations where everything is done for you.
- **Raise the issue.** Everyone knows there are important, unspoken issues, and everyone tends to shy away from them. So brave it and raise the subject yourself. Tell your son that you want to talk about your will or your power of attorney.
- **Defend without defensiveness.** If your daughter wants you to give up your car keys, calmly offer to take a driving test. Or, offer a compromise: you'll drive less and not at all at night.
- **Look for points of agreement.** Even if you disagree with 90 percent of what your children are saying, find points of agreement. That's a good starting point for resolution, and it demonstrates that you are capable of listening and evaluating.[7]

3

Plan Early and
Look Beyond Today

The senior member or members of your family have acknowledged that because of their age, they need some modification in their lifestyles, small or major, either immediately or in the near future. The family supports that decision and says it will do whatever it can to help. It sometimes happens that not all members of the family come to the same conclusion, a subject we'll discuss in Chapter 16. But here we'll assume that the family is of one mind and has accepted your offer to lead the search for the best solution to your parents' needs.

As a first step, we recommend that you, the family team leader, organize a conference of the entire family. A face-to-face meeting would be best, but don't leave a family member out because he or she lives too far away to attend. Keep her in the loop by telephone or e-mail. As team leader, you can get the conversation started, but no one should dictate the agenda or limit the discussion. Also, make it clear to all that the senior who is receiving the care has ultimate control over the plan for his or her future. At this stage, we do not recommend that the senior be involved in the meeting.

The kinds of questions that will come up include these: How do we conduct that search for help for our parents? Who are the professionals we can call upon? What documents do we need? What is the financial impact of the various alternatives? Which alternative is best suited to our parents' health and physical limitations? Which is best suited to their lifelong personalities and current emotional needs?

Start Immediately

We urge you to hold the family conference and begin the search for help as soon as the need, or even the potential need, occurs. In Chapter 5, a helpful box lists a number of signs that indicate that seniors need support. Also, you and your siblings likely sense intuitively that something has changed, however subtly. Your parents are no longer safe without some kind of support. If you wait until your loved one is severely ill, the family might make a hasty decision that everyone will later regret.

Also, as the months go on, it will become more difficult to put together a plan that you and your parents can afford and that will guarantee them the reassuring, secure life that they want and you want for them. There is, of course, the chance that your loved ones will refuse help from you or anyone else. Throughout the book we suggest ways to overcome their resistance. Should you go ahead and arrange help for them even if they insist they don't need it? Maybe not. A colleague of ours and his aunt quietly investigated nursing home options for his mother. When she discovered what was going on behind her back, she was furious, and rightly so.

Take an Inventory and Get Organized

Survey all the resources at the family's disposal, which include people—children, other relatives, neighbors, and friends who will be able to help—as well as crucial documents and financial resources. We'll touch on financial resources later in this chapter and examine them in detail in Chapter 17.

Know where you can find important documents and passwords, bank accounts, retirement accounts, safe-deposit boxes, stocks, life insurance policies, and will and trusts. Make a list of these locations and how to access them, and give copies to at least a couple of other family members. You might be unavailable when an important document is needed. Also, you don't want to arouse the suspicion that only you have access to the safe-deposit box or other valuables.

Do your parents have long-term care insurance? Even if they are in good health, at the age of seventy, it will become increasingly expensive for them to apply for long-term care insurance. So urge them to investigate this option now.

Estate planning is essential. Your parents will want to complete estate planning and collect and organize important documents before they reach a point at which they might be mentally or physically incapacitated. But they keep putting off the meeting with the lawyer. Be respectful, but be persistent until they finally have that meeting.

Prepare to Be Flexible

Understand that, no matter which of the alternatives is chosen among those outlined in the chapters that follow, it is likely that the alternative will have to be modified or even discarded in time. Aging in place or family care may be appropriate for a time, but eventually the senior will probably need professional help as well. So be flexible. It is likely that no resolution will be permanent.

It is quite astounding how much research is required to make intelligent decisions as a senior moves through stages of support. The earlier you and other family members begin collecting the data, the more relaxed and confident you are likely to be around your loved ones. At a time they are increasingly uncertain about themselves, they greatly need your self-assurance.

Join a Support Group

To boost self-assurance, you might want to join a support group for caregivers in your community, or look for one online, such as ElderCare Online's Caregiver Support Center at ec-online.net/Community/Activists/can.htm. There is an abundance of additional information online, ranging from directories of housing facilities to guidance on eligibility for government programs.

Later in this chapter are references to professionals whom you can call upon, in addition to the relatively new specialist in the elder care industry, the geriatric care manager, just discussed. But

What Does a Geriatric Care Manager Do?

A relatively new specialist in the elder care industry is the geriatric care manager, a professional who assists families with problems or concerns they have not been able to handle entirely on their own. These care managers, who usually are licensed nursing or social work professionals specializing in geriatrics, can be especially useful when family caregivers live far away or disagree about care.

Gina lived in Phoenix, and her father, Bill, lived alone in a Los Angeles apartment. She visited him several times a year, and when she noticed he was starting to have some problems managing on his own, Gina called the Area Agency on Aging. The staff helped her set up daily meal deliveries and a home health aide. A few months later, Bill fainted in church and was taken to the hospital. He was there a day before someone was able to track Gina down. The hospital discharge planner wanted Gina to come in person to discuss her father's needs, but she was unable to get away immediately. Her husband suggested hiring a geriatric care manager, someone based in Los Angeles who could keep tabs on Bill. A care manager now visits him once a month and calls Gina with updates and recommendations.

Care managers can evaluate and assess your loved one's needs and coordinate care through community resources. You might also call on them to help lead a family discussion about a sensitive subject. Think of a geriatric care manager as a "professional relative" who is there to help you and your family with identifying needs and finding ways to meet them.

The cost of an initial evaluation varies and may be expensive, but these professionals can offer a useful service. If you decide to look into using a geriatric care manager, the National Association of Professional Geriatric Care Managers can help you find one near your loved one's community.[1]

first, here is some general guidance on the issues and variables that are going to determine the decisions that you and your loved ones make. There are documents that you will need. If you don't have them in hand, ask the senior to assure you that they have been executed and can be retrieved when necessary.

Adult Children Take Note

Ideally, your loved ones should have looked ahead and planned for their declining years, not just their finances, but also how they want to be cared for at the end and how they want whatever inheritance they will leave to be apportioned. However, most people don't prepare as they should. They delay creating wills and advanced medical directives and assigning powers of attorney for reasons that are human and understandable. Those preparations are painful reminders of mortality.

But these are also preparations that caring seniors owe to their children as well as to themselves, even though the seniors have years, even decades, yet to live. And we also know that you, the forty-plus-year-old in good health, are reading the intended subtext here. The preparations you hope your parents have made are ones you should be making now for the protection of your children. We'll return to this subject in Chapter 19.

The earlier in life one deals with the issues, the easier emotionally, because those issues still seem distant and, therefore, less threatening. Also, as many seniors get older, they become suspicious, in some cases perhaps a precursor of Alzheimer's. It is usually easier to talk to a seventy-year-old about a will than to an eighty-year-old.

Estate Planning

Everyone, and certainly everyone with children, should have a formal, comprehensive, in-writing estate plan that designates a power of attorney for someone else to act in their behalf should they become incapacitated; that sets out their wishes for medical treatment at the end of life; that designates a health care proxy when they can no longer make choices on their own; and explains how they want their material estate distributed upon death. You will likely need an attorney for at least some of these documents.

Will. You don't have to embarrass your parents by asking them how they plan to disburse their wealth. Gently explain to them that you simply want to be assured they have wills. If the question startles them, seeing in it a suggestion that they are at death's door, it might help to tell them that you have been remiss as well. You are going to have the lawyer make out a will for you at the same time he writes one for Dad.

Even when the financial consequences of dying without a will are small, the emotional repercussions can be tremendous. When Mom dies, who is going to get the antique ring she loves so much, Marla or Doreen? Mom should stipulate in the will that Doreen gets the ring and Marla the special china. Otherwise, Marla and Doreen may get into a battle that will separate them for a long time. It can actually be a great satisfaction for Mom to sit down with Doreen to tell her why the ring is so right for her and to tell Marla why the china is so perfect for her. Then, Mom must put her selections in writing.

Your parents should also put in writing how they want their remains disposed of. Do they want a traditional funeral and burial or cremation? Do they have special requests for a service? Again, we know these are unsettling questions, but someone will have to make decisions. If Mom and Dad don't, the children will, and that process can lead to unpleasant, emotional quarrels among siblings. Appeal to your parents on this level: we all want to be assured that after our deaths, our family members will go on, united and loving one another.

Advance Directive. This document, sometimes referred to as a living will, is another that everyone should prepare, no matter what his or her age. The document states the signer's wishes in case some terrible accident or medical episode leaves him near death with little or no chance of recovery. Does the patient want artificial feeding and respiration? Or does he decline any attention other than liquids and pain relievers? Or something in-between? The same document, or an additional one, creates a health care proxy, a relative or friend who can make decisions about retaining doctors, say, or moving the patient to another hospital or helping the hospital staff interpret any ambiguities in the advance directive.

Power of Attorney. The senior should give someone the power of attorney to act on his behalf if he is disabled in an accident or by an illness. Even though he will likely recover to take care of his own finances and sign important papers, in the meantime someone will have to write checks to pay medical bills, have the lawn mowed, and sign the lease on the summer cabin he is renting out. If Dad gives you and your brother joint powers of attorney to act on his behalf, make sure the document allows either one of you to act independently. When you're writing a check on Dad's account to pay the telephone bill or similar routine item, it's an unnecessary nuisance to have to wait for your brother's signature as well. For major transactions, however, it would be wise to have both your brother's signature and your own on the check or document. That will give you some protection from second-guessing by other members of the family.

Finances

Finances will likely be a major determinant of the kind of care the senior will receive over the years as he moves from stage to stage (see Chapter 17 for an in-depth discussion on financing care).

Asking your father for a look at his investment portfolio or recent income tax returns is as ticklish as asking him about his will. At this juncture, you might suggest to your parent that the family invite a trusted outsider, such as an attorney or a close friend with a good sense of personal finance, to join the discussion.

Unless the senior is in an immediate physical or mental crisis in which a decision has to be made immediately, the tone of these meetings should be relaxed and reassuring. You and other family members should emphasize that this is long-range planning of the sort any adult should be thinking about, including the young members of the family.

How much does Mom and Dad's income amount to, including social security, pensions, rentals, and the rest? What are the assets, and how liquid are they? Stocks and bonds generally can be turned into cash immediately. The six acres your parents own by the lake will likely take much longer to sell.

Just because you have agreed to lead the investigation to find out what's best for your loved ones, it doesn't mean that you have to do all the legwork. Break off a chunk of it and assign it to a sibling or your father's sister.

Insurance. Sorting through the various insurance options can be a major task. Do the seniors have life insurance policies? Do they have medigap policies (private insurance to bridge the gap between costs covered by Medicare and those costs for which seniors are responsible) so that they are protected from large out-of-pocket costs?[2] You'll want to be aware of what Medicare will or will not pay when specific situations arise, such as if your father is rushed to the hospital with a stroke or other affliction.

You'll also need to consider what happens when he is discharged and sent home or to a nursing home and he needs medical care. For instance, Medicare covers skilled care in a skilled nursing facility under certain conditions for a very limited time.[3] Does he meet those requirements? Does Dad have long-term care insurance, which is distinct from medigap insurance? Long-term care insurance does not supplement Medicare; it picks up certain expenses after Dad goes home or to a nursing facility and Medicare stops paying.

Long-term care insurance is expensive and, for obvious reasons, increasingly so the older the policyholder is when he first signs up. Beyond the age of seventy it may be difficult to initiate such a policy at any price. (Another advisory to adult children: sign up for long-term care insurance while you are still in your fifties and policies are relatively inexpensive.) You'll want to understand the answer to another question: under what circumstance will Mom or Dad qualify for Medicaid, the government insurance that pays nursing home bills and some others after the patient has exhausted his or her own means?

Will Children Contribute? How much are you and your siblings willing to pay for the care of your parents? Be realistic and a little hard-nosed about this. Let's assume that you will become the primary caregiver and will have to drive across the city four or five times a week to feed them or help with the housework. Gas is expensive. Perhaps it is not realistic to ask your parents to reimburse you.

But it might be appropriate to ask your siblings to pay for your gas and other out-of-pocket expenses. If you don't ask them for help, you're going to be fuming at yourself while you're caught in one of those inevitable traffic jams: "I have to do all the work. And I have to pay for it." Even if you earn twice as much as your brother, make him pay. It's in his best interest, because if you feel put upon, your parents will sense your anger and be upset. That's not what your brother wants.

Also, always keep in mind that as time-consuming and energy-draining as the duties of caregiver are, they are also very gratifying experiences that you can enjoy in the moment and also look back on with warmth and satisfaction after your parents have passed away. Don't stand in the way of your siblings and other family members deriving similar benefits as caregivers. Encourage them to help, not simply out of a sense of duty, but also for present and future gratification.

Geography

Geography is a critical factor in choosing among the alternatives for care. If you or your siblings live close to your parents, family care may be an attractive choice. But what if you and the others have all moved away, or if your parents have moved to Arizona?

Based on our experience, long-distance caregivers can be helpful no matter how far away they are. This might involve figuring out what you can do to help Aunt Lilly sort through her medical bills or making the most of a weekend visit with Mom.[4] According to a study from the National Alliance for Caregiving and AARP, 15 percent of family caregivers live one or more hours from the person for whom they are providing care.[5] Almost half of long-distance caregivers devote nearly one full working day a week to managing their loved one's affairs.[6]

The survey polled 1,100 long-distance caregivers, although not necessarily primary caregivers, who lived an average of 450 miles away on the frequency of their visits to loved ones under care. Despite the challenge of long travel time (an average of more than seven hours one way), half of those surveyed managed to visit their loved ones at least several times a month.[7]

As a long-distance caregiver, you might find yourself arranging for in-home care, helping your parents move into a new home or facility, or acting as an information coordinator by helping aging parents understand the confusing maze of home health aides, insurance benefits, and durable medical equipment.[8]

Geography is important for other reasons. How close is the nearest major hospital to the senior's residence now and to any residence he might transfer to? Can he get to shopping, the movies, the health club, the church, and the senior center by foot or public transportation, or will he need a car? How much will Dad's arthritis restrict him or Mom's diabetes confine her? Your parents should ask their physicians for an assessment of the likely decline they might suffer as a result of any ailments they have.

Finally, Mom or Dad's temperament will be a major consideration in deciding what kind of care he or she will need. If Dad is an introvert, he will probably not be happy spending his days at a senior center. If Mom is an urban woman, she might not be happy in a country setting, no matter how serene and lovely it looks to you.

You have made it through a demanding chapter, one that has asked you to collect and evaluate a large and varied amount of data. The following chapters will be somewhat simpler in that they will ask you to focus on only one alternative at a time.

4

Aging in Place

The odds are great that your parents will want to stay in the familiar surroundings of their own home and not move anywhere else permanently, not to a condominium in Florida, a retirement compound in Arizona, or a nursing home across town. Most people want to remain among children, grandchildren, friends, comfortably worn furniture, often-traveled streets, and shops where the staff knows them by name and preference. Some 70 percent of seniors spend the rest of their lives in the place where they celebrated their sixty-fifth birthdays, according to one survey.[1]

Still, there are some important barriers to seniors remaining at home, even while they are in pretty good physical and mental health. They can no longer climb stairs with the ease of forty-year-olds. Their balance is not as sure as it once was, so they worry about slipping on throw rugs or, especially, in bathtubs. Arthritis makes it difficult for them to get a good grip on standard round doorknobs.

Your parents like to go out to dinner but don't feel confident driving at night anymore and don't want to depend on you to chauffeur them all the time. They could walk to a couple of restaurants, but as older people, they feel somewhat vulnerable on even familiar streets after dark. Perhaps most important, they feel increasingly lonely. Some of their friends have passed away or moved, and they are not sure how to create a new network at this stage of their lives.

Fortunately, recent innovations have made what is called "aging in place" much easier, safer, more practical, and more enjoyable for seniors who remain at home. Among those advances are *universal design*, a way of designing and building homes that people can live in with ease throughout their lifetimes, regardless of their age; imaginative new technology that can keep track of older people while they are living alone and detect deviations from their routine behavior that suggest an accident or onset of illness and then direct a rescue team to the home; and networks of seniors in the same geographic area who share services, everything from food shopping and exercising together to arranging access to doctors, gardeners, and tax experts.

Universal Design to Make Living Easier

With the retirement of 78 million baby boomers now getting under way, the National Association of Home Builders (NAHB) has given more thought to creating a house that will last a lifetime, that is, one that will be easily habitable no matter what the age of the occupants or their handicaps, such as difficulty with sight, hearing, or mobility. Universal design is intended to accommodate such needs.

If you are at the stage of life in which you are considering the hire of a contractor to build a new home for yourself, think about some of the features you might eventually want as you get older, for example, extra-wide door frames for the easy movement of wheelchairs and a built-in ramp alongside the front step for the same purpose. Interestingly, those same universal design features are also useful for the easy movement of baby carriages, as well as desks and file cabinets for the home office.

You want a full bathroom with a shower rather than a tub on the ground floor, near a room that may start as a playroom but can eventually be turned into a bedroom. The track lighting and windows should be placed so they illuminate places where older people might slip or simply need brighter light for reading. The kitchen should be equipped with a super microwave oven to cut down on the use of gas and electric burners by sometimes forgetful seniors. For more information, consult the Center for Universal Design, online at design.ncsu.edu/cud.

Now let's return to your immediate concern, an easy-to-live-in house for Mom and Dad or other seniors in your life. If they plan to move to a smaller home or one closer to children or friends, ask the real estate agent to help find a house with univer-

> ### Ten Questions for a Senior to Ask Herself About Aging in Place
>
> How important is . . .
>
> - being close to family and friends?
> - staying near familiar places (stores, restaurants, entertainment)?
> - cost to decisions about making my home safe and comfortable?
>
> How comfortable would I be . . .
>
> - living in a new surrounding?
>
> What are my plans?
>
> - Is this a long-term destination where I plan to spend the rest of my life?
> - Is this a temporary/intermediate living arrangement?
>
> About my living choice . . .
>
> - Has it been constructed according to universal design principles?
> - If not, can it be adapted for universal design?
> - How much can I afford to modify a home?
> - How much am I willing to invest to make a residence aging-friendly?

sal design features. More home builders are finding that there is a good market for homes built specifically to accommodate the special needs of seniors. Even if you cannot find the complete universal-design home, keep in mind that some houses are more easily adapted than others to the safety and comfort of seniors.

Anticipate Safety Concerns and Make Improvements

More likely, the seniors will want to stay in the home they have lived in for many years, and the odds are that their home was not built with senior compatibility in mind. However, there are many improvements that can be made in the house immediately, some very inexpensively. (See the box later in this chapter on what $500 will buy.) Your first challenge may be convincing them that such adaptations are necessary. "We see a lot of seniors who don't want to admit they're getting older, so they don't want to make changes in their homes," says Danise Levine, assistant director of the IDEA Center at the SUNY Buffalo School of Architecture.

Convince them that it is necessary. Point out that the U.S. Centers for Disease Control and Prevention estimates that one-third of all accidents that befall seniors could be prevented if homes were adapted to safeguard their well-being. Unfortunately, many adaptations made to the home are responsive rather than proactive, observes Peter Bell, president of the National Aging in Place Council, an advocacy group dedicated to helping seniors remain at home. "Too often changes aren't made until someone has had a stroke or some other condition that impairs his mobility," notes Bell. "That's a difficult time to be making a renovation."

Choosing a Contractor and Making Room Priorities

Another impediment to getting seniors to remodel their homes is their fear of being ripped off by contractors who are either dishonest or incompetent, says Dan Bawden, owner of Legal Eagle Contractors in Houston. So Bawden, in cooperation with the NAHB and the AARP, developed a program to train certified aging-in-place specialists (CAPS). Through the CAPS program, remodelers take a three-day course to learn the business and ethics of remodeling for seniors.

Suggest to your parents that they contact a local CAPS-trained remodeler to adapt their home. (Visit the NAHB's CAPS website, nahb.org/caps, to locate one in your area.) It would be a good idea to consult an occupational therapist knowledgeable about your parents' vulnerabilities as well.

Bathrooms. The bathroom is the most dangerous place in the house, says Bawden, especially getting in and out of the tub or shower. One remedy is to take out a tub and convert it to a shower with no or low curb, which can be done for as little as $5,000. Add a handheld flexible showerhead as well.

Putting in rubber strips, nonslip tile, or similar flooring in the bathroom can prevent a lot of falls. Higher toilet seats are also easier to rise from. A CAPS remodeler will almost certainly recommend grab bars, not only for the shower and toilet, but for other hard-to-navigate places in the home, including the front door and steps in and out of a sunken living room. Tip: be certain that the height of the bars from the floor matches the height and size of the seniors.

Also check the water heater's temperature, making sure that the water doesn't get hot enough to scald. A plumber can easily reset this if it's too high.

Doors and Lighting. Bawden also suggests lever handles on both doors and faucets throughout the house. "I often recommend higher wattage lightbulbs in hallways and bathrooms," Bawden continues. "People my parents' age, children of the Depression, try to save money on low wattage lightbulbs, but it is not worth the increased risk of falling this creates." He also urges seniors to get rid of the throw rugs at the bottoms of the stairways, which are easy to slip on.

Kitchens. Kitchens are risky because of the potential for burns. "Recently I was in a sixty-year-old house occupied by a woman

What Will $500 Buy?

Home Instead Senior Care has compiled a list of inexpensive fixes to make life safer and easier; prices are approximate and may vary by vendor and region. Large hardware stores, lumberyards, stores specializing in remodeling, and websites that carry adaptive equipment stock many of these items.

- Raised toilet seat with arms that lock onto an existing toilet to provide height and support, $90
- Handheld shower nozzle that fits over a tub faucet, $24
- Floor-to-ceiling grab bar that provides a full range of heights to hold onto while sitting or standing up (it's a good idea to install one by the bed, one in the bathroom, or one by a favorite chair), $150
- Lever doorknob turner adapters that attach securely to a variety of round doorknobs to provide leverage for easy opening, $22
- Lever handles that attach to recliner chair handles to serve as an extension, $22
- Various kitchen items are available, including automatic openers that remove lids and open cans, jars, and bottles, $50
- Rubber ramps, which are often easy to install to most surfaces (these ramps stay in place by their weight and can be moved from one opening to another), $36
- Mobile stools, which are particularly useful to help seniors navigate kitchens, $100

with dementia," says Bawden. "There was only one electric outlet in the kitchen, behind the burners of a gas-top stove. It would be very easy for her to catch a sleeve on fire while reaching over a burner. I recommended getting rid of the outlet." As with the bathroom, seniors can scald themselves if the water temperature in the kitchen pipes is set too high. Call a plumber to install a fixture, which enables that a safe maximum temperature be reset simply by adjusting a screw behind the wall plate.

Use the Latest Safety Technology

Ingenious high-tech devices to safeguard seniors while they live at home are coming on line with increasing frequency. Most of us are familiar with the personal emergency response system (PERS). A senior living alone wears a pendant or wristwatch with a button she can push in the event of an emergency that signals a call center to dispatch a rescuer. The alert system can also include high-quality phone connections between the senior and the center. A new sister system includes a phone that prompts the street number on the senior's porch to illuminate and flash when she dials 911, making it easy for a rescue team to find her house.

One of the most advanced new systems is based on a series of sensors and motion detectors placed in strategic spots in a senior's home. With a sophistication that sounds like something out of a high-tech espionage movie, the eNeighbor[2] remote monitoring technology tracks and learns the senior's typical daily activity as he opens and closes kitchen cupboards to have his meals, sensors on medicine containers keep count of usage, and sensors on beds can tell when he gets in and out. If the senior deviates from his usual pattern, a call center is alerted. Another application of the eNeighbor system is early identification of Parkinson's disease. Sensors in the floor or under the rug can help detect the telltale change of gait that signals the disease long before other symptoms. Consult your certified aging-in-place specialist for assis-

Robots to the Rescue . . . Someday

Japan, a longtime leader in robotic technology, is turning its attention to creating humanoid robots that have the potential to help persons with disabilities and the country's burgeoning senior population.

For instance, Toyota has created what it calls the i-foot, an egg-shaped easy chair supported by two humanoid legs that in one demonstration scooped up a human model into its seat and gracefully swept her across the floor; the model controlled the i-foot with a joystick.[3] And experimental engineers at Waseda University have devised a four-legged robot about the size of a large, headless dog that can easily ascend and descend a stairway with a person on its back.[4]

For now, these amazing robots are much like the concept cars often put on display in auto shows. They are a long way from production. Still, it is not impossible to imagine the day when robots will help the elderly and disabled move around their homes and neighborhoods in comfort and with confidence.

tance in installing these or finding a trustworthy vendor who can do so for you.

Aging in Village: Networks of Services

OK, so let's assume that you're ready to make modifications to the senior's home to make it safe and livable for years into the future. Then, before making the investment, there are other considerations to evaluate: Is the community in which the house sits senior-friendly? Is the environment safe? Are there the basic services—groceries and pharmacy to mention just a couple? It does little good to have a perfectly adapted house without taking into consideration other factors that make the community and environment a friendly one in which to live.

A movement that shows great promise for supporting and supplementing the adaptation of the home to the changing needs of seniors is the aging-in-village initiative. This movement encourages healthy seniors in a neighborhood to form a network of services and activities to both help and entertain one another with programs they have created themselves.

A pioneer in the movement is Beacon Hill Village in the heart of Boston, founded in 2001 with the stated purpose of enabling a growing and diverse group of Boston residents to stay in their neighborhoods as they age and lead safe, healthy, and productive lives in and around their own homes. It currently boasts 480 members, ranging in age from fifty to ninety-nine, who get discounts from approved and vetted local dog walkers and pet sitters, computer geeks, personal trainers, gardeners, home helpers, cab drivers, plumbers, tax experts, and painters, among others. Beacon Hill Village also sponsors a variety of weekly programs, which sometimes include a walking group, stretch class, exercise group, personalized grocery shopping, discussions of current events, conversations on film, and a Tai Chi class.[5]

The aging-in-village movement is growing but not yet established throughout the country. To find out if there is a village within your loved ones' area, contact Beacon Hill Village at beaconhillvillage.org, which maintains a list of villages around the United States.

Naturally Occurring Retirement Communities

A companion movement to the aging-in-village strategy is the naturally occurring retirement community (NORC). A NORC differs from a "village" in that it is not self-organized and self-funded. NORCs are sponsored by government agencies, both federal and local, and philanthropic groups. Members have some

How One Village Works

A decade ago Susan McWhinney-Morse, who is now seventy-five, and ten other residents around Boston's historic Beacon Hill began to think about how they could continue to live in their beloved neighborhoods into old age. Friends were not encouraging. "You can't retire there," McWhinney-Morse recalls their warnings. "It's cold and steep. There are bricks and stairs." Also, many of the traditional community institutions had gone, such as the neighborhood grocery and the doctor who pays house calls.

But McWhinney-Morse and her cohorts persevered. They dug deeply for information about the community's demographics, topography, services, and remaining institutions and how to access all of these assets. "We became a consolidator of services," she explains, the go-to organization for those over fifty who needed help of any kind. Members can access any kind of service imaginable. Beacon Hill Village is a virtual community made up of 480 members scattered over a few square miles. Annual dues, which range from $600 for singles to $850 for households, support a small office and staff of five.

One of McWhinney-Morse's favorite services is food catering. Not long ago she had knee replacement surgery, and when she returned home from the hospital, she discovered she had three houseguests, her husband's cousins. "I thought I couldn't cope with being a hostess," she says. "But then the doorbell rang and there was dinner." The caterers had been alerted. "And it wasn't expensive," says the relieved Bostonian.

voice in programs but are not autonomous. NORC members are likely to be older with lower income overall than village members.[6] A housing-based NORC can be located in an apartment building, a housing complex with multiple buildings under common management, or an area where a number of apartment buildings are clustered together. A neighborhood-based NORC is typically located in a neighborhood of one- and two-family homes.[7]

A model NORC is the Lincoln Square Neighborhood Center on the Upper West Side of Manhattan in New York City. More than 800 people aged sixty and older live in thirteen high-rise buildings and a small cooperative apartment house nearby. A major objective of the Lincoln Square NORC is to make certain members have access to health and medical facilities. The NORC staff helps provide members with twenty-four-hour-a-day access to primary health care. Medical case management is available for those who are homebound.[8]

There is a social side to the NORC as well. It sponsors yoga, aerobics, and dance classes, as well as shopping and entertainment excursions and trips out of town. Currently found in many U.S. communities, NORCs are expected to become more common as the population ages.

Happily, the resources that help seniors age in place without constant supervision from you and other caregivers are considerable and growing all the time. At some point, however, seniors may have to move up to the next level of care, family care, which we will discuss in the next chapter.

Aging in Place

Aging in place enables seniors to live safely and comfortably in their own homes or other primary residences. This option utilizes some or all of the following: special housing design for seniors, the installation of safety and convenience equipment, and services that enable the senior to remain at home.

Advantages
- Maintains familiar environment
- Fosters community continuity
- Maintains valuable social networks
- Provides cost savings over other options
- Strengthens families
- Promotes physical and mental well-being
- Naturally occurring retirement communities (NORCs) provide opportunities for residents to band together to access services

Disadvantages
- Low to moderate investment in home equipment and home modifications, but the cost can be high depending upon the extent and nature of modifications performed.
- Lead time may be lengthy (weeks) for determining need, finding a contractor, and completing modifications for individual home remodels outside a village environment.
- Without home modification, structural barriers in the home may present challenges and contribute to falls and injuries.
- Seniors may be resistant to home modifications and the installation of helpful technology.

(continued)

Choose This Option If
- Senior is functional on all activities of daily living (ADL), which include: eating, bathing, toileting, dressing, maintaining continence, and transferring (getting out of a bed or chair)
- Limited assistance is required by senior
- Prospect is good for sustained independent living

Average Annual Cost
- Varies, depending on what support services and equipment are needed

Resources Available
- For community-based services, check with local Area Agency on Aging, n4a.org
- National Aging in Place Council, naipc.org
- SeniorResource.com, seniorresource.com/ageinpl.htm
- Aging in Place Initiative, aginginplaceinitiative.org
- Center for Aging Services Technologies, agingtech.org/about.aspx
- American Association of Homes and Services for the Aging, aahsa.org
- National Association of Home Builders with certified aging-in-place specialists, nahb.org
- Sources for a certified aging-in-place specialist, nahb.org/caps
- To learn about universal design, design.ncsu.edu/cud or ap.buffalo.edu/idea
- Beacon Hill Village, beaconhillvillage.org

Issues You Should Be Aware Of

- Certified aging-in-place specialists—trained and certified by the National Association of Home Builders—are knowledgeable in addressing the special needs of older people.

When It Is Time to Move On

- It is no longer safely feasible for the senior to remain at home.
- More skilled or professional senior care services are necessary to enable the senior to live safely at home.
- More frequent or around-the-clock supervision is needed.
- Significant medical assistance is necessary.

5

Family Care

Your parents put you at the center of their lives for your first two decades. They hovered over your sickbed, worried about your school grades, and stretched their finances to send you to college. So it is entirely natural and appropriately symmetrical for you to want to take care of your parents in their final years. Repaying benefactors, especially the ones you love most, is one of the most gratifying experiences humans can have. You can fulfill the promise, explicit or implicit, that you will always keep your parents close by and never abandon them to a nursing home as a first recourse or unless it is the best care alternative. Spending an extended amount of time with your parents can also be great fun, reliving old times, accumulating new ones. But, mostly, it is about honoring your mother and father.

Nevertheless, the responsibility of being a primary caregiver can overwhelm you, especially if you have other duties, such as a job or your own young children. The time requirements and physical demands of caring for older people are taxing. The emotional ones can be even more so. Overseeing your awkward toddler as he gets stronger every day may be exhausting, but it's also exhilarating. Watching your aging father get weaker every day, angrily so, is not.

Signs That Family Care Is Needed

So before you agree to become the primary family caregiver, think through all of the likely consequences carefully.

The family care alternative often appears as an option when aging in place is no longer adequate. Your parents are still capable of carrying out all the functions of daily living, such as dressing, grooming, eating, toileting, and moving about the house. But Mom or Dad now need at least some regular help. How do you know? Here are some of the signs:

Look in the refrigerator, freezer, and drawers. Has food spoiled because Mom can't get to the grocery store? Does she have dif-

Seven Questions Before You Decide

If you become the primary caregiver . . .

1. Are you prepared for the pressure on your spouse and children?

2. Have your spouse and children agreed to take Mom or Dad into your own home?

3. Have you established a working arrangement with siblings and other family members?

4. Have you anticipated the wear and tear on your own health?

5. Are you prepared for the emotional stress of long-term caregiving?

6. Have you evaluated the financial cost of providing family care?

7. Will you be able to continue working *and* provide family care?

ficulty cleaning tight, cluttered places? Look over the grocery list. Has Mom's declining health prompted her to purchase more convenience and junk foods and neglect proper nutrition? Is she losing weight?

Look through the mail. Is Dad's dementia causing him to forget to pay bills and answer correspondence? Look below bathroom and kitchen sinks. Is poor eyesight making it difficult for your elderly relative to read medication labels and to properly store cleaning materials?

Is Dad forgetting to refill medications and to take them on schedule? Check the refill date against the number of pills in the bottle to help determine if your loved one is taking medication regularly. Or call the pharmacy. Look at your senior's appearance. Is clothing dirty and unkempt, and is your loved one neglecting personal hygiene?

If the answers to these questions raise concerns, your senior probably can no longer live entirely on his or her own. Throughout the book we'll discuss the various options available for help, but in this chapter we'll focus on just one of them, family care.

Varieties of Family Care

Family care can take a number of forms. According to recent research done by Home Instead Senior Care, just over half of those seniors under family care remain in their own homes alone. Often they are widows or widowers. One or more family members drop by to help with chores or simply to check on the senior's well-being at least once a week. In another 20 percent of the cases, a senior couple lives together, an arrangement that provides companionship for both, although it often puts a great burden on the healthier of the two.

The Senior Lives with the Family

In addition, a familiar lifestyle of the nineteenth century, the multigenerational household, is making a comeback in the twenty-first century. In bygone years, it was common in much of the world, including the United States, for middle-aged couples to live in the same household with their aging parents, as well as their young children.

According to a 2008 survey conducted for Home Instead Senior Care, 43 percent of adult caregivers in the United States ages thirty-five to sixty-two reside with the parent, stepparent, or older relative for whom they or someone else in their household provides care. In fact, the multigenerational household is now the fastest growing living arrangement in the nation, although the number of households in this category is still small—according to the 2000 U.S. Census, about 3.9 million (or slightly less than 4 percent of all households).[1] Professionals in the real estate and building industries believe the trend is accelerating as the population ages.

The multigenerational household is the most complete form of family care. An elderly parent moves in with his children, or less commonly, the children and grandchildren move in with him.

The Senior Stays in His Own Home

In an alternative and much more common form of family care, the senior stays in his own home, but one or more members of his family make daily, or at least frequent, visits to help prepare meals, help with housework, and drive him to the doctor or his

---

Family Care May Be Needed When . . .

- spoiled foods remain in the refrigerator
- foods on the shelves are past expiration date
- the kitchen or bathroom has become unsanitary
- the normally neat house is cluttered
- there is a lot of convenience or junk food in the house
- Dad is rapidly losing weight
- unpaid bills are piling up
- other correspondence goes unanswered
- out-of-date medications are accumulating
- Dad's appearance is becoming unkempt
- Mom's personal hygiene has deteriorated

"Where Is My Wife?"

Elizabeth is only twenty-one in chronological years, but she's much older in terms of compassion and wisdom. For several years while attending school full-time and working part-time, she has also been the primary caregiver for her elderly grandparents. Her grandmother suffered a plethora of ailments, including cancer, strokes, and broken bones. Her grandfather had Alzheimer's. "Where is my wife?" he asked Elizabeth one evening. "She's in the hospital, Grandpa," Elizabeth replied. "She had a stroke. Remember?" He didn't, even though he had been with her in the hospital all day.

The emotional strain of days like that one would have felled many secure and seasoned adults. But Elizabeth has been able to handle the burden, along with the physical chores of taking her grandparents to doctors' appointments, weekly shopping, and the rest. At times she feels overwhelmed but still rewarded. She has come to realize how much there is to learn from people who have lived as long as her grandparents, and also to appreciate her own agile body and working mind as gifts that will someday vanish. "People tell me there is a new sensitivity in me since I began caring for my grandparents," says Elizabeth.

chess club. An enormous number of Americans provide this service for the elderly and can be considered caregivers, some 44 million Americans, according to one survey. Almost half of them are taking care of a spouse. Viewed from a different perspective, statistics indicate that almost one-quarter of all households in the United States contain a caregiver.[2]

Three Generations Benefit

The appeal of family care is spiritual, in part. Compared to some alternative forms of care, it keeps seniors in close contact with their offspring, often to the benefit of three generations. Children get the satisfaction of paying back with love, moral support, and sometimes financial aid what their parents have given them over the years. Grandchildren get a unique opportunity to learn family history firsthand.

Financial Cost of Family Care

Family care is relatively inexpensive, at least compared to professional care. Those 44 million Americans mentioned earlier who provide some care to seniors perform services that would cost $257 billion a year if performed by paid caregivers.[3] Unpaid caregivers have some out-of-pocket expenses, however, and those can be considerable. In one survey, the highest expenses were incurred by caregivers who had to travel long distances to visit the seniors. The average annual cost for that group was $8,728, nearly twice as much as the cost for caregivers who lived nearby.[4]

Those caregivers who live in the same home with the seniors under care estimated on average their costs at $5,885 a year for such items as additional food, other household goods, transportation, medical care co-payments, and pharmaceuticals. This adds up to 10 percent of the median income for family households in the United States, which is $59,894. The costs are even higher when it's necessary to modify a household with ramps and railings, by widening doorways, and in other ways rearranging a household to accommodate seniors with even minor handicaps. On top of that, many caregivers have to cut back their work hours, and therefore their pay, to stay home and tend to the needs of an increasingly infirm senior.[5] This also can affect the caregiver's long-term earning potential, retirement, or social security.

Offsetting those extra costs—and in many cases surpassing them—are the monthly Social Security payments, pension, and other income the senior now contributes to the household. So it's clear that every family's financial balance of additional expenses and additional income will have to be computed individually. If you are the prospective caregiver, or care receiver, take time to do the calculations beforehand and do so in consultation with the rest of the family. It will minimize misunderstandings and arguments later on.[6]

Families interested in making a thorough analysis of the cost of family care or comparing the relative costs of Mom moving in versus caring for Mom in her own home will find the financial calculator on Home Instead's makewayformom.com website very valuable.

The real cost of family care, however, is more likely to be emotional and physical than monetary—and that is generally true whether the senior remains at home or moves in with the caregiver.

Nonmonetary Costs of Family Care

No matter how much the caregiver loves the recipient, the task of caregiving can be extraordinarily draining. The caregiver who has young children at home is constantly pulled in one direction by a child who has to be driven to baseball practice and in the opposite direction by a mother who has to go to the doctor or physical therapy.

Young children and aging seniors are more likely than others to need hurried trips to the emergency room or doctor's office from time to time. The addition of one more person into the household is likely to interrupt routines the household has held as sacred for years. A caregiver can live with a persistent sense of guilt that she is cheating someone of time, space, attention, and love. And, most often, she ends up neglecting her own sense of well-being.

Anticipate Problems

Grandpa is frying eggs on the kitchen stove, and the kids, in a rush to get to school, aren't able to fix their breakfast. Grandpa complains that the kids' friends are noisy, and admittedly, they are. By inviting your father into your home, you now have a permanent weekend guest. Identify as many potential problems as you can before a senior arrives, and talk them out with the whole household.

The family caregiver who has to cross town, or the state, to take care of Grandpa has a different set of problems. There is no fighting over who gets to use the kitchen and when, but the time lost in traveling to Grandpa's house has to come from somewhere—a movie with your husband and kids, lunch with friends, your exercise workout, your sleep perhaps. And then there's the anxiety that overtakes you when you're caught in traffic. Will Grandpa be upset or worried because you're late? Will he try to make dinner for himself and cause you to fret that he'll burn himself or forget to turn the stove off? In the past he's forgotten to turn the stove off afterward.

Pay Attention to Stress

There's just no getting around it. When you choose to become a family caregiver, your quality of life will change. Recent data from Home Instead Senior Care research suggests that quality of life for family caregivers is 50 percent lower than that for all adults. Caregiving also decreases general happiness and health.

Roughly one-third of family caregivers complain about their inability to find time for themselves, the difficulty of managing emotional and physical stress, and the challenge of balancing work and family responsibilities.[7] According to one survey, caregivers report chronic conditions at nearly twice the rate as noncaregivers. Nonetheless, despite their ailments, they get to go to the doctor only four times a year, compared to seven for their noncaregiver counterparts.[8] The reasons for their relative lack of medical help are not evident, although it's possible they simply have less time to take care of their own health.

Almost two-thirds of caregivers have had to make adjustments to their work schedules, such as reporting late or, in extreme cases, quitting entirely.[9] As a national phenomenon, the stress of

Caring for the Caregiver

Here are some tips on taking care of yourself:

- Give yourself a break. Have a team of siblings, other relatives, or neighbors take over your responsibilities at least one week a month.
- Keep a pile of 3″ × 5″ index cards handy. Jot down your needs. When someone asks how she can help, hand her a card.
- If you've never used the Internet before, start now. There are a lot of websites with useful information.
- It's hard to find time for exercise, an antidote to stress. Be creative. While you're waiting for Mom at the doctor's office, walk up and down the stairway of the medical building, which is great aerobic exercise.
- Meditate. When you feel you are overwhelmed, break away for half an hour or so, sit still, and breathe deeply with your mind as quiet as possible.

Family Care

The family bears the entire responsibility for taking care of the elderly person—either in the senior's home or in the home of the family member.

Advantages
- Fulfills the "promise of home"
- Opportunities for close personal relationship with your senior
- Low cost of care (primarily out-of-pocket)
- Great personal satisfaction
- Intergenerational bonding

Disadvantages
- Risk of high personal and family stress
- Potential for multigenerational conflicts
- Possibility of underserving the needs of your senior
- Neglecting your own family
- Loss of productivity on your job

Choose This Option If
- Senior is functional on all activities of daily living (ADL)
- Limited assistance is required by senior

Average Annual Cost
- An estimated $5,000 to $8,000 in out-of-pocket expenses to provide care, including transportation, meals, etc., but depends on the care situation

(continued)

Resources Available
- National Family Caregivers Association, nfcacares.org
- Home Instead Senior Care's CaregiverStress.com website
- Lotsa Helping Hands, lotsahelpinghands.com
- A Place for Mom, aplaceformom.com
- Work Options Group, workoptionsgroup.com
- Family Caregiver Alliance, caregiver.org
- Children of Aging Parents, caps4caregivers.org
- *How to Care for Aging Parents* by Virginia Morris (Workman Publishing, 2004)
- *The Parent Care Conversation* by Dan Taylor (Penguin Books, 2006)
- *Parent Care Solution* by Dan Taylor (AuthorHouse, 2004)

Issues You Should Be Aware Of
- Family care is the most rewarding and demanding option
- Loss of job productivity
- Loss of income
- Stress in family caregiving can lead to elder abuse

When It Is Time to Move On
- Personal stress reaches high level
- Family relationships are strained
- Senior needs more and more specialized care

elder care is likely to grow. By some estimates, members of the baby boom generation, the leading edge of whom are now a few years past sixty, are likely to spend more time caring for elderly parents than raising children.[10]

One of the great ironies of family caregiving is that in seeking to maintain the independence of your mother, you may sacrifice your own independence.

What's more, the average family caregiver has been at it for four years. And, the typical caregiver who lives nearby spends more than twenty hours per week caring for her mother.[11]

The Ultimate Gift

For most, family caregiving is a labor of love. According to recent Home Instead Senior Care research, nine out of ten family caregivers have chosen to provide family care out of a love that's rooted in respect for family and driven by the urgency of ensuring Mom gets the best care possible in spite of the physical, emotional, and financial cost to the family caregiver.

Before agreeing to take on the responsibility of being the primary caregiver, think through all of the ramifications, or as many as you can. Caregiving is full of surprises. Over time, many caregivers will not be able to handle the burden on their own and will have to call upon professional help, which is the subject of the next chapter.

6

Senior Centers and Adult Care Centers

While your parent is living at home, either his own home or perhaps yours, two excellent types of community centers can provide him or her physical exercise, social interaction, and intellectual stimulation for hours during the day. At the same time, these places, the *senior center* and the *adult care center,* can provide you, the caregiver, a needed break from your rewarding but demanding responsibilities. The two terms are sometimes loosely interchanged, and there is some overlap between them. But there are significant differences as well, and it would be a discouraging experience for your loved one to wind up in the wrong center.

Senior centers are for those who are in good mental and physical health and may be as young as fifty-five. Healthy seniors seek a place where they can take part in activities like reading books and magazines, attending classes on gardening or pottery, working out on fitness machines, and dining in the company of their peers.

Adult care centers, on the other hand, are for those who have age-associated disabilities, such as physical frailty and early-stage dementia. They may be getting professional care at home but can come to the adult care center as well during the day, where they receive valuable physical and mental stimulation.

We explain the two in sequence in this chapter. To locate both kinds of centers in your area, contact the U.S. Administration on Aging's Eldercare Locator at 800-677-1116 or visit eldercare.gov.

Senior Centers

The first senior center opened in New York City fifty-nine years ago, and the number of centers across the country has ballooned to 15,000, which means that there is almost certainly a senior center in or near your community. Not only do senior centers provide social and recreational outlets for seniors, they are also a great repository of information on aging and provide support for family caregivers.[1]

Because the seniors who attend these centers are in sound physical and mental health, it is generally the senior himself or herself who takes the initiative in joining, for the convenient meals or the opportunity to socialize and participate in a variety of activities. Perhaps the senior has heard about the center from the family caregiver, but he might as easily have learned from a friend or perhaps an advertisement. Generally, he drives himself to and from the center and puts together his own activity schedule. The assumption of self-sufficiency is an element that distinguishes senior centers from adult care centers.

Many of the senior centers are supported and funded at least in part by state and local governments and such nonprofit organizations as the YMCA, United Way, and religious groups. Often the only expenses that the seniors themselves have to bear are the modest costs of lunches or other meals. Close to 10 million older Americans now use a senior center from time to time, and undoubtedly more would join if they could get over the perception that senior centers are not for them.[2]

Maintain Social Connections

At their best, senior centers are great resources, especially for widows and widowers whose social circles may have shrunk with the loss of their spouses. Even though they may not acknowledge it, they need the social, intellectual, and physical stimulation of being around other people. Some experts believe that the challenge of learning a new skill, be it landscape painting, yoga, or a new language, may help delay the onset and progress of Alzheimer's.

Unfortunately, some senior centers have lapsed into drab routines that reinforce their reputation as being knitting klatches for very elderly women. Active seniors shun them. Experts note that attitudes of seniors about their own age often play a role in

Senior Centers and Adult Care Centers: Know the Difference

Senior Centers
- Clients must be in generally good mental and physical health.
- Major focus is interaction with peers.
- For seniors who are interested in activities.
- May offer skill training, education, and information programs.
- Flexible participation and use policies; drop-ins welcome.
- No contracts or minimum participation requirements.
- Generally operated by community, local government, or not-for-profit organizations.
- Fees and costs are generally limited to meals.

Adult Care Centers
- Generally intended for seniors with age-associated disabilities.
- Accept clients with physical frailties.
- Accept clients with early-stage dementia.
- Offer programs with mental and physical stimulation.
- May offer medical services.
- Generally operated by not-for-profit organizations.
- May be associated with assisted living centers.
- Seniors must be ambulatory.
- Seniors must not be severely cognitively or physically impaired.
- Seniors must be continent.
- Source of respite care for family.
- Fees may range from $25 per day to $100 per day.

whether they want to participate in a senior center. Some don't see themselves fitting in with the senior set.

That's why many centers are changing the way they look and feel with a younger focus on health and exercise classes and computer centers.

Look for Baby Boomers

Look for centers that are being rejuvenated by the arrival of the older baby boomers, that is, those who are entering their early sixties. As a generation, the boomers have always been demanding, sometimes annoyingly so, but in this case, their insistence on their rights and preferences is to the advantage of the senior community in general.

Boomers will not put up with centers that offer nothing but bland food and endless rounds of bingo. They want, among other things, Pilates classes, courses in conversational Spanish, and Wi-Fi in the library so they can connect to the Internet through their laptops. If the seniors in your life do not require Wi-Fi, they can nonetheless benefit from the excitement of being around people who challenge their minds with new ideas.

Many centers emphasize health and wellness, listening to what participants want and relying on them to help run the center.

In some of the larger centers, early retirees arrive mornings to exercise or line-dance. Afterward, they have coffee with their classmates, whose ages range up to the mid-eighties and whom they find inspiring.

Adult Care Centers

These gathering places are designed to provide social and some health services to adults who need supervised care in a safe place during the day. Generally, they are open five days a week during normal business hours, although some offer evening and week-end programs as well. Nationally, there are far fewer adult care centers than senior centers, only 3,400 or so, providing care for about 150,000.[3]

ACCs are as much a source of respite care for the family care-giver as they are a protected, comforting gathering place for seniors. For many caregivers, the ACC is the place to drop Dad off for a day so that the family caregiver can rest, handle impor-tant family matters, go to work, socialize with friends, go to the doctor or the movies, shop, or play golf. Without this resource,

Family Respite Care

When John's Alzheimer's disease progressed from simple for-getfulness and confusion to increasingly childlike behavior, his wife and adult children realized that it was impossible for him to remain at home around the clock, seven days a week. For his well-being, he needed to be engaged in social activities outside the home and with people other than family. And the family needed a break as well, especially his wife, who was stretched to her limits by the demands of caring for John along with the other realities of life.

At first, the family was reluctant to turn to an ACC for help. After all, wasn't it her responsibility to take care of John? But it was still the best alternative for the time, so they enrolled him in an ACC recommended by friends and the Department of Vet-erans Affairs. John was not entirely happy in the new setting at first, but in a few weeks, he began to enjoy it. He liked the attention the staff gave him and the opportunity to bowl and dance and sing as he had done when he was younger. His favor-ite days were those on which the Humane Society brought dogs and other pets to stroke.

many caregivers would be locked into caring full-time for a loved one. Fittingly, ACCs are generally quite flexible. They can pick up the senior, or the caregiver can deliver him, every weekday, several days a week, or simply as needed.[4]

The surroundings in an ACC are by and large pleasant, but generally they don't have the stimuli and clubhouse atmosphere of a top-notch senior center. They are deliberately low-key, because the participants are less active than those at senior centers. More than three-quarters of adult care centers are run by nonprofit organizations, some associated with larger organizations like skilled nursing facilities or medical centers. Most ACCs provide transportation to and from the participant's home.[5]

"Nonprofit" does not mean that they are free to users, however. Rates range from $25 to more than $100 a day, partly dependent on how much care the senior needs. If the center specializes in health care services, government programs may pay some of the fees. Also, some long-term care insurance policies provide for care in ACCs.[6]

Who Are ACCs For?

Who should attend an adult care center? You know that your loved one is probably in need of an ACC when she can no longer structure her daily activities by herself and can't safely be left at home alone. Even if she could take care of herself at home, she wants human companionship and can benefit from it. You have to go to work, and there is no family member or friend who can fill in for you while you are away.[7]

The ACC can be a stimulating and supportive place for Mom to spend the day, once she is persuaded that it's a good fit for her. A senior might not be willing and eager to go to an ACC, though. That's especially true if the loved one has medical or cognitive problems. That's why it may take a gradual introduction to the center. When seniors are feeling secure, they will enjoy this respite from home, as will their caregivers.

Some experts advise families to seek out ACCs that are small and therefore quieter and less intimidating to new participants. That's a fair observation. However, consider this: over the age of eighty-five, there are more than twice as many women as men.[8]

If the senior you are seeking placement for is your father, he could find himself the only male in a small ACC. He wants to talk about the NFL playoffs, but all the conversation around him is about grandchildren. In a larger ACC, he might find a few like-minded males.

Levels of Care

ACCs generally accept seniors who are physically or cognitively impaired but not so limited or impaired that they require constant supervision, as someone with advanced Alzheimer's might be, for example. They must be physically mobile, at least with the assistance of a cane, walker, or wheelchair. Most centers also require that participants be continent.[9]

Finding the right ACC might prove more difficult than finding a senior center. As noted previously, there are far fewer ACCs. Also, the participant has to be matched with the appropriate program among the following three kinds that ACCs offer, and not all ACCs offer all three programs.

■ **Social day care** is for those who are not suffering from any serious physical or mental handicaps but are no longer physically robust nor mentally acute enough to function confidently and independently in a senior center. They want companionship and to play board games, sing in a group, discuss their favorite TV shows, and lunch together, but they need the supervision of psychologists or other aides to keep the group activities from falling apart.[10]

■ **Health day care** at an ACC helps seniors with a range of physical and medical needs, such as making certain they take their medications and stick with their physical, speech, and occupational therapies (helping them with grooming and dressing themselves and other skills that may now be impaired). The ACC provides nursing services and sometimes incontinence care as well. An important objective is to keep the participant functioning at the top of his or her physical and mental range.[11]

■ **Dementia day care** serves those with Alzheimer's, Parkinson's, Huntington's, and other conditions causing dementia, although not with the symptoms of advanced dementia, such as combativeness or wandering, which might require constant one-on-one care. The staff for this service has to be highly trained in dementia care, have good communication techniques, and be able to manage difficult behavior with gentle understanding.

Loving and reliable dementia day care is an extraordinarily valuable service. Families who have to care for dementia victims on their own are generally under great stress. Having an ACC that can take some of the burden and assure family caregivers that there will be times during the week they can relax and turn their attention elsewhere is a tremendous relief. It can mean the difference between the senior staying at home and moving to more advanced care with more professional services and supervision.[12]

Call the Centers

Once family members, and probably the family physician as well, have determined which of the three levels of care Mom is going to need, the next step is to call centers in your area and ask for brochures, monthly activity calendars, menus, and applications. Find out how long the centers have been in operation and whether they are licensed or certified, if that's required in your state. What are their fees? What's the ratio of staff to participant?

What impairments do they accept? Severe memory loss? Incontinence? Limited mobility?[13]

Next, visit the centers you find attractive, and look and listen carefully. Talk to the staff and to participants to get a feeling for what it would be like to spend several hours a day in that setting. Be sure to ask for references from other caregivers. Presumably, you are near the beginning of a continuum of care that may someday progress to assisted living quarters or a nursing home. At that point, you will definitely want references. So treat the application to an ACC as a learning process as you become a more experienced care manager.[14]

Linger for a Time

Once you have chosen the ACC that is right for your mother and have enrolled her, keep in mind that entering an ACC is at least a mildly traumatic experience for her. Almost certainly you were the one who initiated the enrollment, not her. Especially if she is entering a dementia care center, she might have feelings of abandonment. The first few times you take Mom to the ACC, linger for a time to get a sense of whether she is adjusting. Later, visit the center at least several times while she is there, to provide reassurance that she is not being dumped and pushed out of your mind and life. It will also give you an opportunity to see firsthand how well the ACC is run and how well your mother fits in.[15]

Be Careful on the Next Move

At some point during your mother's attendance at an ACC, it might become clear that she needs more intensive care. She can no longer take part in even mild physical activity, perhaps doesn't move from her chair all day. Or perhaps her dementia is becoming impossible for the staff to control.[16]

Senior Centers and Adult Care Centers

Senior Centers
Generally operated by communities, local governments, or non-profit entities, these are places where seniors (who live independently) can gather on a daily basis to eat meals and to engage in social, fitness, and creative activities.

Advantages
- Regular social, intellectual, and physical stimulation
- Nutritious meals and snacks
- Many are currently updating physical facilities and programs with computers, fitness activities, and educational courses

Disadvantages
- Seniors may find offerings to be uninteresting, unsatisfying
- Participants' differing demographic groups may cause some to feel "they don't fit in"

Choose This Option If
- Senior is in good mental and physical health and lives independently
- Senior is primarily interested in activities and interaction with peers

Average Annual Cost
- Daily fees are nominal, typically limited to meals

(continued)

Resources Available
- U.S. Administration on Aging's Eldercare Locator, eldercare.gov
- National Association of Area Agencies on Aging, n4a.org

Issues You Should Be Aware Of
- Senior centers assume that members will be self-sufficient.
- Typically, this includes seniors transporting themselves to these locations.

When It Is Time to Move On
- Senior is becoming more frail or is dealing with an increased number of age-associated disabilities
- Senior needs supervised care during the day, including social and some health services
- Senior is in early-stage dementia

Adult Care Centers

These are community-based group programs designed to provide social and some health services to adults who need supervised care in a safe place during the day.

Advantages
- A safe, secure environment
- Socialization, educational activities, and support for seniors
- Enhanced or maintained level of independence
- Nutritious meals and snacks
- A source of respite for family caregivers
- Some centers offer social, health, and dementia day care

Disadvantages

- Senior may feel frustrated/abandoned
- Facility may not be as good as it appears
- Facility might not meet senior's individual needs
- Finding the right fit might be difficult

Choose This Option If

- Senior can't be safely left alone at home
- Senior can no longer structure own daily activities
- Senior is isolated and needs socialization
- Senior is in early stages of dementia or Alzheimer's disease

Average Annual Cost

- Daily fees for adult day services vary depending upon the services provided (the national average rate for adult day centers is $61 per day, eight to ten hours a day).

Resources Available

- National Adult Day Services Association, nadsa.org
- National Association of Area Agencies on Aging, n4a.org

Issues You Should Be Aware Of

- The three most common types of ACCs are (1) social day care, (2) adult day health care, and (3) dementia day care

When It Is Time to Move On

- There is an increase in special care needs (incontinence, wandering, sleeplessness, and combative and other difficult dementia behavior)
- Senior needs care that extends beyond the normal workday
- There is a decline in physical health of the caregiver

This is a time when you, the caregiver, should be alert to what's going on. As mentioned above, some ACCs are affiliated with assisted living facilities and nursing homes and are, therefore, sometimes feeders for those institutions. This is not necessarily bad, but you should understand it is a possibility. The ACC staff may advise you to move Mom into the assisted living or nursing home the ACC has a relationship with. That may well be the best thing, but be aware of any vested interest the ACC might have in such a move, and take that into account as you make your decision.

You have alternatives. A better solution may be to keep Mom at home and supplement your own care with professional help. We'll talk about that in the next two chapters.

7

Nonmedical Care at Home

At the point that you'd consider nonmedical care at home, your parent has likely, with some help from you and other family members, created a support structure that has been sufficient for mental and physical health. Mom or Dad has remained at home and has maintained a moderately active social life outside, gone out to dinner and a movie with friends, revisited nearby vacation spots.

But now it is becoming apparent that some additional one-on-one care may be needed beyond what you have the time and energy to provide. You are likely seeing signs that your mother or father is losing the ability to manage her or his own life. You may notice a tall stack of unopened mail on the desk. The cable

Ten Signs of Trouble

The Home Instead Senior Care Advisory Board has compiled this list of indicators that your loved one may need additional companionship.

1. **Household bills piling up.** Seniors can feel overwhelmed by the simple task of opening and responding to daily mail, as well as balancing a checkbook.

2. **Reluctance to leave the house.** Rather than ask for help, seniors who are having trouble with such functions as walking, remembering, and hearing will pull away from their community and isolate themselves.

3. **Losing interest in meals.** Seniors who suddenly find themselves alone, perhaps after the death of a spouse, can be easily discouraged by such tasks as cooking and tend not to eat properly.

4. **Declining personal hygiene.** Changes in appearance, unkempt hair and body odor, failing to change clothes for days on end, or clothes inappropriate for the weather are among the most obvious signs that a senior needs assistance.

5. **Declining driving skills.** Look for evidence of parking or speeding tickets, fender benders, dents, and scratches on the car.

6. **Scorched pots and pans.** Cooking ware left forgotten on top of an open flame may be a sign of short-term memory loss or even Alzheimer's disease.

7. **Signs of depression.** Feelings of hopelessness and despair, listlessness, fewer visits with friends and family, a change of sleeping patterns, and lack of interest in the usual hobbies and activities are indicators of depression.

8. **Missed doctors' appointments and social engagements.** These can be signs of depression or forgetfulness. But they can also be the result of no longer having a driver's license and not knowing how to get alternative transportation.

9. **Unkempt house.** Changes in housekeeping may come about because the senior is physically tired. They could also result from depression.

10. **Losing track of medications.** Seniors often take multiple prescriptions for various health conditions. Keeping track without reminders and assistance can be confusing.

Source: "10 Signs a Senior Relative May Be in Trouble," from Home Instead Senior Care's Caregiverstress.com website, caregiverstress.com/extrainfo .html (accessed March 10, 2009).

company is threatening to cut off her TV service, and she can't understand why. But it's clear to you that she hasn't paid the bill. Your father, traditionally very circumspect about his appearance, goes for a week or so without shaving; his slacks are rumpled, evidently a pair he has been wearing for a couple of weeks. (See the box "Ten Signs of Trouble" in this chapter.) If there are enough signals of this kind, you begin to wonder if your parent or parents can continue to live at home unassisted.

Determined to Stay Home

What is your next step as the family caregiver? Do you suggest a move to an assisted living facility? That's probably not the best solution, certainly not immediately, but we'll discuss such facilities in a later chapter. For now we'll just point out that it is an expensive option. Moreover, it is almost certainly not the option your parents would choose, for they are probably among the large majority of seniors research shows who are determined to stay home.

Your parents' preferences need to be taken into account. Even though they are not as sharp as they were in the prime of life, your parents have not lost the right to help shape their destiny. This chapter and the next discuss options available to help keep Mom or Dad safely and comfortably at home and to keep everyone's anxiety level to a minimum.

Moreover, there is generally no compelling need to move a senior into a facility at the stage when just nonmedical help or often even light medical help is needed. "Unless the senior is on life support, he can get almost any treatment in his own home, and he is better off because there he can get one-on-one attention," says Sheila McMackin, president of the National Private Duty Association (NPDA).

Considering a Professional Caregiver

It is worth noting this kind of in-home nonmedical care can be as important and effective for your mom if she is now living in a care facility as if she were living at home. Depending on your circumstances, it may not be possible for you to make regular trips to visit her in a care facility. Her circle of friends is likely shrinking and—most likely—they have transportation challenges of their own. So she may be lonely. Or the staff of the assisted living facility where she lives is so stretched that you are concerned about the extent of her interaction with others. In either case, the solution may be a caregiver companion—someone who can provide just the basic support she may need to make staying home a viable option. This could include assistance with meal preparation and light housekeeping but can include services such as transportation to medical appointments, entertainment, or shopping. Many times, an in-home nonmedical care service will offer just old-fashioned companionship—someone to visit with about old times or today's news or hobbies.

Caregiving Outside the Home

Nonmedical caregivers can provide their services at places other than the clients' homes. A high school principal in the Midwest found a place in an assisted living facility for his seventy-five-year-old mother who was suffering from dementia. She did well there, but the supervision was relaxed, and at night she was inclined to wander. Her son worried that she would stroll outside on a frigid winter night and not be found until morning. So he hired a caregiver to pass the time pleasantly with her during the night and keep her from a fatal wandering.

Although in this chapter we focus on the services professional caregivers provide in the client's home, they can also take on the role of comforter in assisted living quarters and nursing homes. In nursing homes, a caregiver hired by an individual client encourages the client to eat and drink and stay alert and engaged in conversation and games, functions the nursing home staff are unable to provide because they are so busy with daily routines and responding to patient crises.

Remember You Are Trusting a Stranger

Perhaps you would love to bring your parents into your own home and care for them exclusively on your own, but your job, the needs of your kids and husband, the space you have available, and other circumstances won't allow it. The solution is to find professional caregivers to come into your parents' home to help out. Finding those professionals is perhaps the most important and potentially risky assignment you will have as a family caregiver. You are asking a stranger to take care of your parents.

Moreover, the stranger is not doing so inside an institution, whether that be an adult care center (ACC), an assisted living facility, or nursing home, where there are supervisory structures on the premises. In an institutional setting there is some risk that an individual caretaker may be neglectful—or careless or even abusive—but that caregiver is generally monitored by supervisors, who can correct or discipline her or put another caregiver in charge.

But the stranger who comes into your parent's home to help is for the most part working alone. For hours of the day, it will be just her and your mother or father. Even if the caregiver has the best heart in the world, she may be entirely ignorant of fundamental health care information, such as the signs of a possible stroke or heart attack. Or she and your mother may simply have a serious personality clash, which may cause your mother great stress. Particularly if your parent has dementia and can no longer identify and articulate the source of the stress, you may have no idea what is troubling her. Or, you may fear that her complaints are not valid because her memory is faulty and she may have some degree of paranoia.

Caregivers as Friends. We had to give you that warning. But there is a very positive side to the search you are about to undertake. There is an excellent chance that you will find for your parent one of her best friends ever or at least at this phase of life.

The first step is to determine whether your mother needs companionship and some help with personal care and light housework or whether she needs constant medical care that might include

After Many Years of Waiting, He Caught a Souvenir

Paul, an eighty-three-year-old Home Instead client in North Carolina, had seen excitement in his life. He was part of the U.S. invasion force that stormed the beaches of Normandy in 1944 and a lifelong baseball fan. But in all his years of going to baseball games, he had never experienced the thrill that most fans long for, catching a foul ball. One day his caregiver, Stephen, took Paul to a Durham Bulls game.

The game was engaging, but the heat was suffocating, so in the seventh inning they got up to leave, Paul disappointedly empty-handed one more time. As they were leaving, they heard the familiar crack of a bat, looked up, and saw the ball floating overhead. It landed at Paul's feet. His face lit up in amazement. On the way home, Paul tossed the ball back and forth between his hands in quiet delight. "Maybe you can come back some time and we can have a catch," Paul suggested as he and Stephen parted. "It would be my pleasure," Stephen replied.

someone to administer oxygen or blood transfusions or intravenous drugs. Or something in between. You might want to consult with your parent's physician, a geriatric care manager, or a local member of the National Private Duty Association (NPDA) to help you decide. If your mother needs medical care, such as someone to check her blood pressure and heart rate, to make sure the respirator is working, or to manage infusions or administer medications, we will discuss the right kind of professional for her in the next chapter.

Looking for a Caregiving Companion. In this chapter, we assume that your parent needs basic support, which will allow her to stay safely and comfortably in her own home. Simple companionship, someone to talk to and socialize with, help with light housework and personal care, such as with bathing and dressing, and car transportation to and from shopping and other nearby destinations might be all you need right now—the things you would do if you could give up the rest of your life.

At this point we want to repeat the disclosure that we made in the Preface. This nonmedical home care is what Home Instead Senior Care, the organization founded by the authors of this book, provides.

Costs and Schedule

Your mother might be confined to home as she recovers from a broken hip or some other surgery. Or her suffering might be more emotional or mental than physical. Your father died six months ago, and she is understandably depressed, lonely, and unsure as to what she does now that the person she lived with for fifty years is gone. Perhaps she is slipping into Alzheimer's or some other form of dementia.

So you've decided that your parent needs a nonmedical home care professional. She needs someone to engage her in conversa-

"Elderspeak" Hurts

Sometimes the term is "dear," and at other times it's "sweetie" or perhaps "hon" or even "good girl" (possibly spoken loudly and slowly by those who assume all older adults are hard of hearing). Unfortunately, those endearments with which well-meaning caregivers often address seniors are not only cloying and overly familiar; it turns out that they could be dangerous as well.

The language suggests that the senior has returned to infanthood. The senior may unconsciously accept the attitude behind the words as true—you're old, therefore, you're helpless—and that acceptance may contribute to a more rapid decline.

"Those little insults can lead to more negative images of aging," Becca Levy, an associate professor of epidemiology and psychology at Yale University, told a *New York Times* interviewer. "And those who have negative images of aging have worse functional health over time, including lower rates of survival."

Such terms of endearment are part of what is called "elderspeak," a way of diminishing seniors, even though unintentionally. Don't let caregivers talk to your parents like that. Here are some other forbidden phrases: "How are we feeling today?" "How many years young are you?" and, the worst, "Who did you used to be?"

tion, get her to listen to music again, help her plant new flowers in the window box, and bake bread. What can you expect to pay, for how long, and what kind of person would you be able to hire?

Most care of this kind is provided for just a few hours a week. Our surveys indicate that 22 percent of clients employ caregiver services four hours or less per week, and 20 percent employ them between four and eight hours per week.

Mornings might start with the caregiver arriving at the door and urging your mother to get out of bed, take a shower, and change from her nightgown into daytime clothing, as she has done all her life. The caregiver tactfully insists that your mother should have a full breakfast, not just tea. Perhaps your mother needs someone to remind her to turn off the stove. In some cases, seniors need this kind of coaching throughout the day.

This care can be expensive. The national average hourly rate for homemaker/companions in 2008 was $18, according to a survey from the MetLife Mature Market Institute.[1] Therefore, in some cases, the cost of paid care at home could approach that of a private room in a nursing home, which averaged $212 a day in 2008, or that of an assisted living facility, which in 2008 averaged about $100 per day (or $3,031 per month).[2]

But the cost comparison has to be put in this perspective: Where does your mother want to be? What will make her happier? In reality, you won't need twenty-four-hour or even twelve-hour service for your mother at this point, at least. More likely, you'll use in-home nonmedical care for just a few hours a week. About half of the seniors benefiting from this service are using less than eight hours a week, making it very affordable, while helping Mom stay at home where she wants to be.

Overwhelmingly, professional home caregivers are women, primarily between the ages of forty-five to sixty-five. But some are much younger, and others are in their seventies and eighties. Other countries are facing a similar demographic. For instance in

Canada, 80 percent of paid and unpaid caregivers are women, 75 percent of whom are between the ages of fifty and sixty-five.[3]

In the United States, the personal and home care aides classification, of which paid caregivers are a part, is expected to grow by more than 50 percent from 2006 to 2016, increasing from 767,000 to a projected 1.15 million jobs.[4]

The professionals can be grouped into three categories: full-time agency employees, agency contract employees, and freelance caregivers.

What to Ask When Choosing Nonmedical Care

So it's time to consider in-home care. Because this may be the first departure from complete independence or family care, the decisions you make are very important and may color your relationship with Mom and how she sees future care options. You need to make informed decisions about the service you secure and the caregiver assigned to your mother.

Use these questions to get answers as you proceed:

Questions to Ask Yourself
- Does Mom want to stay home?
- Have I discussed this option with Mom?
- Is she open to accepting a caregiver?
- How comfortable will Mom be with a stranger in the house?
- To what extent have you involved your siblings in this decision?
- What kind of nonmedical help does Mom need?
  - Meal preparation?
  - Light housekeeping?

(continued)

- Limited local transportation to doctors and the grocery store?
- Reminders to take medications?
- Companionship?
- Does she need medical support to stay at home? If so, what types of medical services does she need? (Depending on the type and level of care, you may need a different service or to secure supplemental in-home medical service.)
  - Administration of medications?
  - Respiratory assistance?
  - IV drug administration?
- How many hours of service will Mom need?
- How much can we afford to pay for in-home care?
- What will determine how much we are willing to pay?
  - Price of service (hourly rate)?
  - Total cost (for a month of service)?
  - Mom's living preference? (Sometimes home care can be more expensive than assisted living, for example.)

Questions to Ask a Nonmedical Service Provider

- Is the caregiver an agency employee? (This is the arrangement we recommend.)
- Or is the caregiver an agency contract employee? (Make sure you understand the implications.)
- Or is the caregiver working on her own/freelancing? (Be wary.)
- Have the caregivers been trained?
  - By whom?
  - What is the extent of training?

- Does this training include special dementia or Alzheimer's training?
  - Does the agency train *all* its caregivers? Are they all trained to the same level?
- Have the agency's caregivers passed criminal background checks?
- Has the agency secured personal references on all caregivers?
- Can you check references on the agency and the caregiver assigned to you?
- Does the agency offer backup/replacement caregivers?
- How much control will you have in selecting the caregivers?
- What restrictions (if any) apply to the services provided?
  - Minimum hours of service per day?
  - Weight restrictions? How much weight will your caregiver be allowed to lift?
- How much flexibility will you have in setting a schedule for services?
- How much notice does the agency need to begin or cancel service?
- What is the cost of service?
  - Is there a minimum number of hours of service per visit/week/month?
  - Are there special overnight rates?
- Does the agency maintain a quality assurance or supervisory program?
- Does the agency provide backup caregivers if your regular caregiver is unable to work?

Full-Time Agency Employees

Home Instead Senior Care is an agency in this category, and we strongly recommend that you pick a professional caregiver from this category. We believe that Home Instead Senior Care and companies like ours are the best home nonmedical caregiving agencies in the business. Our company, and most of our competitors—particularly those who are members of an association—are well intentioned and staffed with competent people. But, as in any industry, there are unethical, shoddy operators, who cut back on services or rely on undertrained and sometimes irresponsible caregivers in order to trim costs and make a larger profit. In picking an agency and ultimately a caregiver, don't hesitate to ask questions about standards and practices.

Be certain that the agency's caregivers are full-time employees who are insured and bonded to cover any damage or injury they might cause persons or property. If an agency you are considering tells you that it is insured and bonded, make sure that the caregivers are covered, not just the agency. Also, caregivers should be screened to make sure they have no criminal backgrounds; they should provide references as well.

Who Trains the Caregivers?

Some states require that the caregiver have received training and be at least a certified nurse's assistant. But we recommend you go beyond that. Who gave the caregiver that training and when? Ask the agency to explain its training program for employees and take a look at the training materials. Does the agency train all caregivers itself? It should. Home Instead Senior Care does so because we feel strongly that it's the only way we can ensure quality. We train caregivers in a four-part program that includes the following subjects: basic care, safety, activities, and advanced care.

For example, one course instructs caregivers in health and safety, everything from how to recognize the onset of a stroke or heart attack to important safety measures. For instance, to prevent falls while climbing stairs, the caregiver should walk behind the client on the way up and in front of the client on the way down. It is important to point out that although a caregiver will help the client with personal care, she will not lift him or her out of and into beds and tubs. For the protection of both caregiver and client, the caregiver is not permitted to lift more than twenty-five pounds.

And another course on how to engage a confused or lethargic client in social activities provides conversational hints about discussing the client's hometown or career. The course even supplies recipes for pie crusts and other dishes to make with the client and instruction on how to line bureau drawers and repot plants. It includes lists of card games and simple physical exercises as well as how to relate to the seniors with whom they work.

Finding the Right Caregiver

Even when you, the family caregiver, have picked the right agency, you are only halfway through your search. Equally critical is finding the right caregiver within the agency. (See the box "Matching Client and Caregiver" in this chapter.) Some combinations are unlikely to work. If either your mother or the caregiver smokes and the other one doesn't, the relationship is probably doomed. Even if the caregiver goes outside to smoke, the smell will be in her clothes. Another frequent barrier is if one has a cat or dog and the other is sensitive to pet dander.

A Language Problem? Fewer than 10 percent of caregivers are male, so the gender issue is not a great concern. A male caregiver and a male client may form an easy friendship. We discourage trying to match a male caregiver with a female client. There are too many occasions of personal care to make that combination comfortable. Many caregivers are immigrants

Matching Client and Caregiver

A caregiver's success is not measured by how many tasks she performs in the hours she spends with your mother; it is measured by the strength of the bond the two of them develop. Again and again, our surveys show that clients value the relationship above all. Don't hurry this process. Your role as family caregiver is to take your time and make sure the professional caregiver and your parent are well matched, no matter how many candidates have to be interviewed.

At Home Instead Senior Care, the process begins when an office representative makes a call to the client's home. Many other companies work in similar ways. Note that the senior under care is always considered the client, rather than you, the family caregiver, no matter who is paying. And, every effort is made to help the senior maintain his or her dignity. The senior is always addressed as "Mrs. Donovan" or "Mr. Sawyer" until the client makes it clear she or he wants to be addressed by first name.

After the initial meeting, the company representative goes through a list of candidates and does her best to pair client and candidate using such criteria as educational background, hobbies, and interests and perhaps religion and ethnicity. Will the client be happy to have the caregiver in her home? That's a critical question. On the next trip, the Home Instead Senior Care representative brings the prospective caregiver along to see whether she and the client will get along. You, or some other member of the family, will almost certainly be present. Resist the very strong temptation to direct the conversation between your mother and the prospective caregiver. If you get actively involved, you will muddy the answer to the question as to whether the caregiver and your mother will bond. Observe what takes place between them. You will, of course, be allowed to express your opinion to the agency representative later. Once your mother has picked her caregiver, you are welcome to check up on them whenever you like. The agency representative will continue to monitor the relationship as well with frequent visits.

whose English is strongly accented. If your mother has difficulty hearing, very common among seniors, understanding the caregiver could pose a considerable problem. On the other hand, if accent and hearing loss are only moderate, they will likely work out an easy conversation pattern within a few hours.

Education Level. Some highly educated seniors, retired teachers for example, want caregivers who can discuss books or current affairs. That's a difficult requirement to fill, although there are some recent college graduates who take temporary positions as caregivers while they are studying for or contemplating other careers. But there are a growing number of well-educated, accomplished professionals who are reentering the job market as caregivers. They are motivated to make a personal and meaningful contribution to the lives of others.

Substitutes. Ask about substitutes when you decide on an agency and on a specific caregiver. Should your mother's caregiver be sick one day, a first-rate agency will have a substitute at your mother's side immediately.

If a Second Caregiver Is Necessary

For most cases, one person can provide the care. But if caregiver attention is required for more than forty hours a week, the agency should assign a second caregiver. Generally, it is not a good idea for a caregiver to move into your parent's home for around-the-clock duty. Like the family caregiver, the professional needs time and a place to get away from her responsibilities. Also, the professional should not come to think of your parent's home as her own.

Agency Contract Employees

In addition, there are contract agency employees, who are typically people who work for an accredited agency that will give back-up support, such as supplying a substitute if they are sick. But this type of caregiver works under contract and is not a full-time employee and therefore may not necessarily have the insurance coverage and other protections for both client and caregiver that a full-time employee would have. That can lead to serious trouble. The contract employee might not have liability insurance to cover any damage she might cause your parent's home. The car she uses to drive your parent to the dentist might not be insured.

There are also tax ramifications. If for example, your mother brings into her home a caregiver who is a contract employee rather than a full agency employee and pays her more than $1,600 (the cutoff figure for 2008), *there's a chance* your mother will be considered the employer and therefore may be responsible for withholding income taxes and paying payroll taxes, and may be subject to workers' compensation liabilities in addition to other legal obligations.

The family of Mildred in New Jersey hired Teresa, an Eastern European caregiver who was working in the United States legally on a visa but who was unfamiliar with American law. The agency failed to withhold federal taxes for Teresa, who was shocked when she discovered that she would have to send the IRS $5,000 she did not have. Mildred's children paid the taxes, partly out of compassion and partly because they didn't want to demoralize and alienate a caregiver who had developed a fine bond with their mother.

Freelance Caregivers

Freelancers are caregivers who work independently without any agency affiliation in what is sometimes referred to as the "gray market." Perhaps she was recommended by someone in your office or a neighbor who used her services when her own mother was sick, or it could be a family friend or the lady next door.

The biggest advantage of using a freelancer is that she is almost certainly the least expensive of the three alternatives. There is no business organization and staff behind a freelancer that also has to be compensated. She might work for the federal minimum wage or some other compensation agreement, and she might do heavy housecleaning as well.

The disadvantages and dangers are considerable, however. For a start, if you pay her more than $1,600 a year, you may be responsible for withholding her taxes and providing workers' compensation.

The freelance caregiver may have no training in how to be a companion to the elderly. Who, other than you, supervises her? Does she know about safety standards? Does she understand the medicines your mother must take and when? Would she be able to recognize the onset of serious illness? Whom does she call if she needs help? Who substitutes for her when she gets sick? What if she walks out the door halfway through a shift because she has been offered a better job? What if she takes your mother's jewelry with her?

While there are many caring, capable people who work freelance, we cannot recommend you go this route because of the dangers. If you do choose this alternative, be certain that the freelance caregiver comes with references you trust without question.

The Beginning of a Beautiful Relationship, Ideally

As you finish this chapter, you should have a good idea of what to demand in nonmedical care for your loved one. At its best, the relationship between professional caregiver and senior can blossom into a wonderful friendship. The caregiver can help bring back your mother's talents for cooking, flower arranging, decorating, and music that you had long forgotten about. Going through family pictures with your mother, she may help your family discover parts of your mother's life you weren't even aware of.

Your mother can thrive at home for a long while with the help of a nonmedical caregiver. But what happens if she gets sick and needs medical attention? Must she leave home? Sometimes, yes, but not necessarily. In the next chapter, we'll look at the medical services that can help your mom maintain her independence with a medical illness.

At-Home Care

Home care combines health care and supportive services to help homebound persons continue living at home safely, comfortably, and as independently as possible. The hours, types of services, and level of care provided are determined by the health and needs of the care recipient and the primary family caregiver. Nonmedical home care services include companionship, light housekeeping, meal preparation, medication reminders, errands, shopping, and, in many states, personal care.

Advantages
- Provides individuals needing care with dignity and independence
- May help prevent or postpone hospital or nursing home care

- Allows maximum freedom and comfort for the individual
- Offers individualized care tailored to the needs of the senior and family
- Provides professionally supervised services
- Supports families while keeping them together

Disadvantages
- Standards and practices vary among nonmedical home care companies.
- While more and more long-term care insurance companies are covering this option, it is still primarily private-pay, and costs may be prohibitive for some.

Choose This Option If
- Senior is functional on all activities of daily living (ADL), although many nonmedical companies are licensed to provide personal care
- Only limited assistance is required by senior
- Senior is mobile and able to benefit from staying at home

Average Costs
- $15 to $25 an hour depending on geographic region and size of community

Resources Available
- U.S. Administration on Aging's Eldercare Locator, eldercare.gov
- National Private Duty Association, privatedutyhomecare.org
- Home Instead Senior Care, homeinstead.com
- National Association of Area Agencies on Aging (check locally or visit n4a.org)

(continued)

Issues You Should Be Aware Of

- Are a minimum number hours per visit (usually three to four) required?
- Does the company conduct minimum criminal background checks on caregivers as well as secure personal references?
- Are the caregivers trained to provide caregiving services?
- Does the company bond and insure caregivers?
- Is there a system that provides for backup care?
- Does the company provide a daily log or other means to report what happens in the home?
- Does the company have a process to resolve problems or issues?
- Have you determined the employment status of your caregiver? Is she employed by the agency? Or is she your employee, in which case you may be responsible for payroll taxes and workers' compensation?

When It Is Time to Move On

- It is no longer safely feasible for the senior to remain at home.
- Care needs become greater than either nonmedical or medical support can provide.

8

Medical Care at Home

E ven if their daily living skills have declined, your parents can remain in their home safely and happily with professional nonmedical care, as we described in the last chapter. But what happens if one of them suffers a severe medical trauma, such as a stroke, a broken hip, or surgery that requires him to be fed intravenously afterward? Under those circumstances, will he have to go to a nursing home to recover?

Not necessarily. Over the past couple of decades, many life-enhancing and lifesaving medical devices have become far more portable and far more adaptable to home use. Everything from x-ray equipment and respirators to walkers and wheelchairs, catheter and wound care supplies, can now be delivered to your parents' home. Moreover, professional medical care agencies can provide teams of nurses, therapists, and other medical aides (and even physicians) to make house calls, set up and operate that machinery, and supervise patients' recoveries. What's more, some of this in-home medical care may be paid for by your health insurance, long-term care insurance, or certain government programs.

When At-Home Medical Care Is Best

As Sheila McMackin, president of the National Private Duty Association, observed in the previous chapter, almost any long-term medical problem can be handled at home, and often better than in an institution. "If you moved someone with dementia to a strange place, he could be two feet from the bathroom and unable to get there," she notes. "At home he knows the route automatically, even with dementia." You also avoid the potential exposure to an infectious disease by staying at home.

If your father suffers a disabling stroke or heart attack, or a broken hip or other trauma, he will likely need follow-up medical care after he leaves the hospital. Other conditions that require medical care are less obvious, so keep his physician informed of changes you think are significant. "Things that might signal the need for medical intervention," says McMackin, "are weight loss, disorientation, new aches and pains that were not there before, bruising from falls, and changes in sleep patterns."

Your conversations with your father's (or mother's) physician can be a very sensitive issue, however. Privacy laws generally restrict what physicians can tell third parties, including family members, about a patient's condition. So ask your father's physician about what he can and cannot tell you and whether he needs a consent form from your father.

Assess New Needs

Over time your father's dementia might gradually progress to the point that he needs more than a caregiver companion to engage him in conversation and make sure that he keeps mind and body fit with a daily routine. He may need a regimen of strong antidepressants and other medications to keep him stable.

Or, his incontinence might become so frequent and uncontrollable that the nonmedical caregivers you have hired are no longer able to cope with it. (Well before he gets to this stage and when you initially interview nonmedical caregivers, be certain you understand the limits of their incontinence care.)

When In-Home Medical Service Is Needed	
• Trauma	• Weight loss
• Disabling stroke	• Disorientation
• Heart attack	• Chronic pain
• Broken hip	• Changed sleeping patterns
• Wound care	• Bruising from falls
• Medication management	• Bedsores (pressure ulcers)

One of the most common—and most dangerous—progressive medical problems among failing seniors is bedsores, technically known as "pressure ulcers." Those who lie in bed for long periods without shifting their position often develop such lesions. They are more than simply painful; they can eventually eat into muscle and bone and even be fatal.

Does She Also Need Nonmedical Care?

One question that comes up frequently is whether an ailing senior requires both professional medical care and nonmedical care. The answer is that in some cases he might. Consider a patient with mild dementia who has fallen and broken a hip. The nonmedical caregiver cannot take care of changing dressings, lifting him in and out of bed, and other major physical needs, all of which a medical caregiver can provide. On the other hand, now more than ever the senior needs companionship and help with making

---

Total Living Choices

When Ted Tanase's sister Jeanne was operated on for a brain tumor and later suffered a stroke and seizures, Ted and his family were stunned and had little time to find help. The hospital gave them a mere seventy-two hours to find a nursing home for her, a challenge complicated by the fact that Jeanne's hospital was in Santa Barbara, California, and Ted was in Seattle. On the Internet, Ted found only lists of thousands of nursing homes with no evaluation of those listed and no guidance on how to choose among them.

Nowhere in pamphlets and books, nor through telephone calls, could he and other family members find worthwhile information about costs of nursing homes and other elder care facilities. Which homes were rated best? Which homes met Jeanne's special needs? (Jeanne was a vegetarian and kept cats.)

The family ran into indecipherable fine print and baffling legalese everywhere. "That we wasted so much time during this period of high stress was inexcusable," says Tanase. "I vowed I would create a user-friendly website so that no one at such a traumatic time would have to go through the frustration, exasperation, anger, and guilt that we felt because of the lack of useful information."

So in 1999, Total Living Choices, tlchoices.com, was born. Free to users, the website offers three programs:

- A care interpreter, which asks visitors to the site questions about the activities of daily living of the prospective resident and then helps to match him or her with an appropriate facility or home health care.
- A home care finder, which helps site visitors find licensed and reliable companies that send professional caregivers to homes.
- A facility finder, which helps families locate quality care communities and facilities. Using industry experts as advisers, TLC has compiled a nationwide list of 50,000 nursing homes and continuing care communities.

The website also offers a care finder for hospitals—the Care Finder Pro—which is helping hospitals locate care options that are allowing patients to be discharged sooner to appropriate follow-up locations. Surveys have revealed that money has been saved and customer satisfaction improved.

"We take away that feeling of helplessness," says Tanase, "and arm consumers with the knowledge and confidence to find the right places for their loved ones."

meals, performing light housework, and such. Those are services in which nonmedical agencies specialize but medical agencies do not necessarily provide.

The medical caregiver's contact with your loved one is likely to be for briefer periods than the regular, warm relationship with a nonmedical caregiver. Once you father's broken hip is healed, the medical caregiver will leave. His dementia, however, will not improve, so the nonmedical caregiver is still essential. Also, as you will see in this chapter, there can be several medical caregivers involved in the treatment of your loved one so that it would be difficult and time-wasting to find a perfect personality match up and down the line.

Relieving the Terrible Fear

A medical caregiver recalled this story for us:

"I'll never forget this client. He was an elderly gentleman who had been incredibly independent all his life. He was blessed with a devoted family but suddenly developed cancer. It came on quickly and unexpectedly, and he went rapidly from healthy to totally bed-bound.

To make matters worse, the client was terrified about dying. So his main caregiver (he had a team of four caregivers around-the-clock) sat on the floor by his bed all night. In short time, the man became so disabled that his caregiver had to sit on the ground and flop him over his shoulder to change his clothes. The two sang show tunes together to lessen the anxiety. With the assistance of intense hospice services and medical care, he was able to spend his last three weeks at home. His caregiver was holding his hands when he passed away."

Without in-home medical care and hospice support, this gentleman would have had no alternative to a nursing home.

Some Advice on Choosing a Medical Care Provider

Seek out a medical caregiver designated a "home health agency," advises James Summerfelt, chief executive officer of the Visiting Nurse Association. "The term often indicates that the provider is Medicare-certified and has met minimum federal requirements for patient care and management." Such agencies are highly supervised and controlled, according to Summerfelt. Medicare covers many of their expenses, and many long-term care insurance policies will pay for much of the rest.

When you interview an agency, make sure you understand exactly what services it will provide and those it will not provide, including those it is forbidden to provide by state law. Families are allowed to provide any care for a family member, but professionals have to abide by state law. For instance, in many states, invasive procedures such as bowel programs and feeding tubes may not be administered by non-skilled professionals. You need a doctor or registered nurse.

According to the Visiting Nurse Association, a home health agency is likely to employ a range of professionals, including the following:

■ **Physicians.** Doctors visit patients in their homes to diagnose and treat them, as they do in hospitals and private offices. They also work with home care providers to determine which services are needed and which specialists are most suitable. The physician then prescribes and oversees the patient's care plan. Under Medicare regulations, physicians and home health agency personnel review those plans at least once every two months.

■ **Registered nurses.** RNs have received two or more years of specialized education and are licensed by individual states. Generally, an RN can administer injections and intravenous therapy, provide wound care, and offer education on disease treatment and prevention and patient assessments, but state

Needed: More Training for the Family

Lynn recalls that after having throat surgery, her father was sent home with a feeding tube. "Not long after he got home, the home health nurse came to the house for the first time to clean the tube," recalls Lynn. "She also used it to give my dad his post-op medication and, because he couldn't eat solid food, a nutritional supplement. The nurse did these things in about twenty minutes. But because this routine had to be repeated several times daily, she needed to train me on it too. Nurses were only going to come by once a day, so someone in the house *had* to know how to do this."

Unfortunately, on one of Lynn's first attempts to give her father his medication, the tube clogged, and what at first appeared to be a simple procedure quickly grew complicated and nerve-racking. Though she and her father used cooperation and instinct to quickly resolve the problem, in her words, "It could have been detrimental to him and his recovery."

Lynn's assessment of the experience: "The home health people did what they're trained to do, which is to provide medical care, and they were good at it. But their visits were 'in and out'— so there was little personal interaction with my dad or with us. To begin with, my family and I really needed more 'hands-on' training. We all could have used more emotional support."

regulations vary. RNs may also provide case management services.

■ **Licensed practical nurses.** LPNs have one year of specialized training and are licensed to work under the supervision of an RN. Whether your parent requires an RN or an LPN depends largely on the difficulty and intricacy of his treatment.

▪ **Physical therapists.** Through the use of exercise, massage, and other methods, PTs work to restore the mobility and strength of patients who are limited or disabled by physical injuries. PTs often alleviate pain and restore injured muscles with specialized equipment. They also teach patients and caregivers techniques for walking and transferring.

▪ **Social workers** evaluate the social and emotional factors affecting ill and disabled individuals and provide counseling. They also help patients and their family members identify available community resources. Social workers often serve as case managers when patients' conditions are so complex that professionals need to assess medical and supportive needs and coordinate a variety of services.

▪ **Speech language pathologists** work to develop and restore the speech of individuals with communication disorders; usually these disorders are the result of traumas such as surgery or stroke. Speech therapists also help retrain patients in breathing, swallowing, and muscle control.

▪ **Occupational therapists.** OTs help seniors who have physical, developmental, social, or emotional problems that prevent them from performing the general activities of daily living, which professionals refer to by the shorthand ADLs. OTs instruct patients on using rehabilitation techniques and equipment to improve such daily functions as eating, bathing, dressing, and basic household routines.

▪ **Home health aides.** They assist patients with such daily activities as getting in and out of bed, walking, bathing, toileting, and dressing. Some aides have received special training and are qualified to provide more complex services under the supervision of a nursing professional.

Medical care at home is becoming an increasingly popular alternative to assisted living and especially as an alternative to nursing homes. It is difficult to say how many seniors are undergoing medical care at home at any one time. There are, however, an estimated 20,000 home care agencies in the United States, and their number is certain to grow with the aging of the baby boomers, according to McMackin.

The advantages of a home care agency are plain. Your loved one does not have to leave the warm and reassuring surroundings of his home of many years. He remains in his community, where family and friends can visit him often and easily. He can stay at home during his final months or years, through hospice care to the end of his life.

Potential Hazards of In-Home Medical Care

A senior's medical condition may deteriorate in a subtle way that escapes the notice of a home health aide, say, who has not been fully trained as a nurse. So it may be a good idea, for example, to plan for periodic visits by a nurse who would easily detect the onset and worsening of bedsores.

The financing of medical care at home is both complicated and confusing. Medicare will pay for many services, such as visits by nurses, and speech and occupational therapists.[1] If your mom is discharged, Medicare will pay for a nurse and an occupational and speech therapist for her at home, but only according to a doctor's prescribed care plan. The goal is to get your mother rehabilitated.

So, although medical care at home, combined perhaps with nonmedical care, is a very appealing course of action for many seniors in failing health, others choose different routes. We'll discuss those in the next chapters.

An in-home care chart is available as a resource at the end of Chapter 7.

9

Retirement and Independent Living Communities

U ntil now we have talked about the care of seniors as they remain in their traditional communities, generally in their own homes, but in some cases in the home of the family caregiver. In either case they are still surrounded by the familiar.

Now we have arrived at a turning point. For the next several chapters, we will talk about seniors who have moved away from their traditional homes. In later chapters, we'll discuss assisted living facilities and nursing homes, but in this chapter, we'll talk about circumstances in which seniors in good health leave their traditional homes.

For the most part, they do so not to turn their backs on their pasts, including friends and family. Indeed, many don't go far away. According to the 2009 Home Instead Senior Care report, only 10 percent of decision makers live more than a hundred miles away from their senior loved one.

Looking into the Future

When seniors do leave their homes, they go for a variety of reasons. In many cases, their traditional homes have simply become too big for them to care for, contain too many rooms to clean and heat, and look out over too much lawn to cut and too much driveway to shovel. Perhaps they have become fearful of crime and want to live in a gated community with private security patrols and restrictions on who may enter. Maybe they no longer want to be around the noise and tumult of young children other than their own grandchildren. They want to play golf, tennis, and bridge in the company of their peers.

Some seniors who move away also take a long look toward the horizon of their remaining years. For now they are healthy, in their mid–sixties, say, but they can imagine the day when they will need a lot of support, including perhaps residence in a nursing home. They want to get in on the ground floor of an independent living community that provides a continuum for the rest of their lives: a complex of facilities that begins with homes suitable for seniors who are fully capable of taking care of themselves. Nearby is a cluster of apartments designed and equipped for those who need some daily assistance, and finally, there is a nursing home for those who need professional caregivers in constant attendance.

Your Role

If your parents are considering a retirement community or an independent living community, they are probably healthy, confident, and competent and not relying on you to take a leading role in finding one for them. That doesn't mean, however, that you can't perform some useful, unobtrusive assistance in helping them find the independent living community that is best for them. For example, you can help them distinguish between communities that emphasize recreational and social opportuni-

Prepare for the Unexpected

Moving to a retirement or independent living community may be your parents' first experience with a community association and its fees. Inquire in advance about the charges for the following:

- Home maintenance and repair
- Gardening service
- Fire and theft insurance
- Snow plowing, trash collection
- Water and other utilities
- Country club membership
- Golf and tennis fees
- Cable TV and Internet access

ties and those that somewhat more soberly stress the support they offer as members of their communities decline either physically or mentally.

You can also help your parents by providing a checklist of questions they should investigate thoroughly before making commitments to a particular community. (See the box "Is This Community for You?" in this chapter.) Pulling up roots is financially expensive, physically exhausting, and emotionally torturous. The experience is punishing enough for a forty-year-old, but for a sixty-five-year-old it is much harder, especially for those who have not lived beyond their home community before. To make a mistake by moving to the wrong place and then trying to undo the mistake by moving elsewhere would probably cause quite a bit of stress that all would rather avoid.

A Great Variety

Hundreds of communities designed for seniors, and in some cases restricted to seniors, are spread across the nation and across a considerable cost-of-living range. Some are luxurious and offer a panoply of recreation and entertainment. Others are modest but still offer basic services, such as bus transportation and housecleaning. Some are communities of houses, others condominiums and apartment buildings, and many are a mixture of all three. A few are in cities, but many more are in suburbs and quite a few in somewhat remote beach and desert areas. Communities go by a number of names, such as senior housing, senior apartments, senior communities, retirement homes, active 55+ communities, and finally, continuing care retirement communities, or life care communities.[1]

Despite the great variety, they tend to cluster around either one of two concepts: recreation or lifetime security. Another way of expressing the difference is active 55+, on the one hand, or continuing care retirement community, on the other. The

> ## About Independent Living Communities
>
> - Typically for the "younger" senior
> - Tend to be oriented either to recreation or lifetime security
> - May be associated with organizations offering accelerated services depending on changing needs
> - Range from luxurious to moderate in cost
> - A variant (continuing care retirement communities) is oriented to provide care over the long term and accommodate changing needs

two concepts are not mutually exclusive, and most communities contain elements of both. The difference between the two is a matter of emphasis. We'll describe two communities that represent the two concepts as a way of helping you and your parents decide which is right for them. We are not recommending either of these communities as being appropriate for your parents. We merely highlight them to help you understand what to expect in similar communities.

Active 55+ Communities

The archetypal community in this category is Sun City, Arizona, a self-contained community of 42,000 about sixteen miles northwest of Phoenix, where the minimum age for the head of household is fifty-five and the average age of residents is seventy-four. Founded in 1960, Sun City has become a national symbol of fun-filled golden years. Amenities include eight golf courses; seven recreation centers with arts and crafts and music venues; three country clubs; two bowling centers; thirty-one churches; sixteen shopping centers; two lakes; a walking pool; and a softball field.

Residents live in both individual, detached one-story houses and apartments. They range in price from $50,000 for a one-bedroom, one-bath unit up to $600,000 (in 2008) for a three-bedroom house on one of the lakes. Property owners in 2009 paid an annual $420 lot assessment fee that allows them to use all of the amenities offered.

The advantages of Sun City are its sunny weather and the great variety of recreational and entertainment possibilities. Because of the large population at places like this, it is generally not difficult for newcomers to find neighbors with hobbies and other interests like their own. "What draws people here is the active lifestyle," says resident Bill Pearson, sixty, who lives with his wife, Lori, in a Sun City home. "Most of us fear getting old," he adds. The liveliness of Sun City seems to help residents forget their fear. "I've started taking classes in the lifelong learning club," says Bill. "Today I gave a speech and then worked out at the health club. My wife spends her days playing tennis and pickle ball." Bill also plans to run for the board of the historical society. Bill's mother, Jane Pearson, was the first to discover the allure of Sun City, after raising a family and braving frigid winters in St. Paul, Minnesota, with her late husband, Will. She's now opted for the convenience of an 850-square-foot independent living apartment.

The disadvantages are that the Arizona sun can be brutal. In July and August in particular, it is not pleasant to be outdoors. So anyone considering Sun City should probably have a retreat in cooler climates for midsummer. Sun City, however, is somewhat remote for those who plan to return often to their previous homes to visit families and friends during those torrid months. "Another drawback for some people is that there are not a lot of young people around," notes Bill Pearson. No one under nineteen can live in Sun City permanently, and grandchildren under nineteen can stay for only ninety days.

Probably the biggest drawback to Sun City is the isolation that residents might experience when they reach the age or condition at which they can no longer travel back to their home communities. Sun City has assisted living facilities and a nursing home, as well as a large and modern acute-care hospital. So residents will be well cared for. But families need to think about whether they and the seniors' friends will be able to visit them frequently.

Back to Birthplaces

Because of the great distance from families and other reasons, many seniors who had moved far from home to retirement communities in bright and sunny areas like Arizona and Florida have decided to move back closer to home. More than 17 percent of older migrants surveyed by the U.S. Census Bureau in 2000 had returned to the place of their birth.[2] Ann's grandparents were living the life many seniors dream of in Florida when her grandmother fell ill. Her grandfather, hard of hearing and suffering from Parkinson's, could no longer care for his wife. So the elderly couple returned to Pittsburgh, where Ann's mother cared for them.

Seniors return from idyllic active 55+ retirement communities for a combination of reasons, including failing health, shrinking financial portfolios, and loneliness for their children, especially grandchildren. The late Dr. Charles F. Longino, Jr., a Wake Forest University professor, called the phenomenon "countermigration."[3]

Family Is Paramount

"Migrants making long distance moves to popular destinations tend to do so after retirement, at the peak of their retirement income, while still married, living independently in their home, and interested in enhancing their lifestyle," observed Longino. "After several years, however, and especially after widowhood and increasing disability, perceptions and needs change. Proximity to family and old friends becomes paramount."[4]

So as your parents contemplate a retirement community, they might want to consider a spot closer to family and traditional roots and one from which they will feel no need to leave if they become frail. It's certainly worth their time to take a look at the many options closer to home. They may find these suit their interests more closely or nearly as well while allowing them to see the people they love more often.

Is This Community for You?

Before seniors move into an independent living community, here are some of the questions they should ask themselves:

- Does the community meet your recreation, entertainment, and social needs?
- Before you buy a home, visit. Is the staff welcoming? Are the residents people with whom you feel comfortable?
- How easy will it be to return to your traditional home for visits?
- What restrictions are there on young children, including grandchildren?
- Is there a gated entrance? Are there security guards?
- Is there an organization for residents to voice views on management?
- How close are medical facilities?
- Is parking convenient to your prospective living unit?
- Is there public transportation?
- Are there a lot of steps and stairs to climb in your unit and elsewhere on the grounds?
- Is your unit equipped with grab bars for the shower and similar aids?

Continuing Care Retirement Communities

CCRCs, sometimes known as "life care communities," have recreational facilities, but their greater appeal is the promise that they will take care of residents for the remainder of their lives. Many have large campuses that include separate housing for those who live very independently; assisted living facilities that offer more support; and nursing homes for those needing constant care. If your parents enter as healthy and fully independent seniors but over time need more and more support, a CCRC will make the transition guaranteed and relatively simple.[5]

An attractive CCRC in Nebraska, for example, is Lakeside Village, which is part of Immanuel Senior Living, a community with campuses in Lincoln, Omaha, and Papillion, an Omaha suburb, that range in size from 70 to 181 residences. The Lakeside Village campus offers independent living, assisted living, memory support (for those with dementia-related issues), and long-term care residences as well. Each Immanuel Senior Living residence includes a kitchen, dining room, great room, bedroom, bathroom, and walk-in closet as well as a walk-out patio or deck. Surrounding them are well-tended grounds with walking paths and in most cases a lake as well.

Residents, who are drawn primarily from Nebraska or nearby Plains states, tend to be upper-middle income, the majority college graduates, many with successful business or professional careers behind them. One eighty-year-old businessman is still picked up by his son every day to go to work. The average age at Immanuel is eighty-two, compared with Sun City's seventy-four. "Over the past five years, we've seen the average age on the increase," said Roxann Rogers-Meyer, Immanuel's director of sales and marketing. "Part of the reason is that seniors are waiting to move, staying a lot longer in their homes before they go to independent living. It's difficult for seniors to leave the home they have lived in for thirty-plus years. They are leaving a life-time of memories that include raising a family."

Residents pay a monthly service fee that includes numerous services and amenities. Unlike Sun City, Immanuel has no golf courses or tennis courts, but it does have among its amenities a restaurant, fitness center, two warm water pools, business center, computer labs, library, barber shop and beauty salon, billiards tables, and an art gallery.

Art Johnson and his wife, Geneva, were longtime residents of Omaha who moved from a townhouse to Immanuel when he was eighty-two and she was seventy-eight. "Geneva was getting tired of cooking," Art recalls. "Also, we knew a lot of people who had strokes or heart attacks and thought it would be nice to be in a place where it's easier to deal with such things. One of the main reasons we came here was the financial strength of the Immanuel system." Their recreational life had once revolved around golf, but it became somewhat quieter when they settled in at Immanuel. Art still goes to the exercise room three times a week, and Geneva goes sometimes as well.

Art is an enthusiastic reader, but also an extrovert who gets together frequently with a crowd of peers who call themselves "the Blue Boys" and sing to the accompaniment of a ninety-three-year-old piano player. Geneva plays bridge. Dinner is at 6:30 followed by a program of some sort and on weekend evenings by movies. Art and Geneva don't leave the campus often, except for family events. Two of their four children live in the Omaha area, which is one of the great appeals of Immanuel for Art and Geneva. Their children can reach them easily. A son drives Art to a Bible study class off campus every Monday.

Art and Geneva have made for themselves a comfortable new life that is not far removed from their old life. If the time comes that they need help with the basic activities of daily living, such as bathing, dressing, grooming, walking, managing medications, toileting, and eating, they can make a simple transition to Immanuel's assisted living facility on the same campus.

There are many other alternatives for assisted living, however, a subject we will discuss in the next chapter.

Retirement and Independent Living Communities

Independent living communities are designed for seniors who are able to live on their own but desire the security and conveniences of community living. These communities are also called retirement communities, active 55+ communities, congregate living, or senior apartments.

Advantages
- Promotes independent living
- Security
- Meals, housekeeping, transportation, and planned social activities often offered
- Senior is surrounded by peers

Disadvantages
- Personal care services usually are not provided
- No formal regulation
- Continuing care retirement communities may require large up-front fee

Choose This Option If
- Senior is healthy and able to care for self
- Senior desires security

(continued)

- Senior no longer wants to maintain house
- Senior prefers to live among peers

Average Annual Cost

- Varies depending on real estate markets throughout United States
- The lowest-cost facilities are subsidized housing, followed by rentals; planned retirement communities are at the higher end
- Monthly fees may apply and can range from a few hundred to several thousand dollars a month

Resources Available

- Alternatives for Seniors, alternativesforseniors.com
- Retirement Living Information Center, retirementliving .com
- HelpGuide.org
- SeniorDecision.com
- Local Area Agencies on Aging, eldercare.gov
- Online guides to independent living communities

Issues You Should Be Aware Of

- Financial obligations and contractual agreements
- Services provided
- Facility's reputation in the community and financial health

When It Is Time to Move On

- Senior no longer is able to care for self

10

Assisted Living

A great and relatively recent advance in the support of seniors has been the development of the assisted living facility, or ALF as it is known to professional caregivers. An ALF can be an attractive option in several circumstances. Perhaps the senior's family lives too far away to provide the support we described in the chapter on family care. Nor does the family feel comfortable supervising from afar professional caregivers attending to their parent's needs at home. Or perhaps the senior requires so much professional support at home that the financial expense of home care has become greater than the family can bear.

As institutions, ALFs lie on the senior care spectrum somewhere between retirement communities, where seniors are mostly on their own, and nursing homes, where seniors are under the constant supervision of nurses and others. In ALFs, help for seniors who have begun to decline physically or mentally is always available on the premises but is not ever-present or overbearing.

"Seniors in ALFs are in need of care, but they want more than anything in the world their independence, and they don't want to be told what to do, when to eat, when to dress, when to get up in the morning, when to go to bed at night," said Rick Grimes, CEO of the Assisted Living Federation of America. They demand their independence because they are adults. But they might wander into situations on the premises that could be dangerous. So ALFs hire staff who can watch from a distance and intervene only when necessary. The level of protection at an ALF is very different from that of both a retirement community and a nursing home.

A Profile of Assisted Living in the United States

According to the National Center for Assisted Living, nearly 1 million older Americans live in about 38,000 ALF residences.[1]

They are generally apartment buildings, where residents live in studio or sometimes one-bedroom apartments. ALFs are outfitted with all of the helpful adaptive devices, like grab bars and ramps, that we described in Chapter 4. Some ALFs do have sections for residents who suffer from dementia and don't leave their rooms often, but by and large, ALF residents come and go as freely as they would at home. There are no mandatory meals, bed checks, or other appointments. Early risers still get up early; sleepyheads sleep late. However, ALFs may come under more regulation and greater oversight, which would impact these and other practices.

Striking Diversity

The diversity among ALFs is striking. "If you've seen one assisted living community, you've seen *one* assisted living community," quips Grimes of the Assisted Living Federation. "There's a lot of pride in our industry in designing communities to meet the needs of the people in the community. Some places are very folksy. Some may be designed around Victorian themes. Some may be modern, contemporary design." (Grimes, by the way, strongly objects to the use of the term "facility," which he associates with people being kept against their will; he prefers "community.")

Some ALFs are affiliated with independent living communities, as discussed in the previous chapter, or with nursing homes. But some are freestanding, without affiliation.

One proprietor we know offers rooms, transportation, meals, care, laundry, and similar services for about a dozen residents in a setting that makes them feel they are still living in a home rather than a care community. The owner and his family build personal relationships with their guests. They play the piano and sing for them, prepare special meal requests, and provide other nice touches.

Mostly Single Women

As we often do in this book, we refer to "your mother" rather than "your parents." Here we do so to help distinguish the ALF experience from that of independent living in the last chapter. In retirement and independent living communities, the residents are likely to be married couples. In ALFs, they are more likely to be single women, especially widows. The typical resident of an ALF is an eighty-five-year-old woman.[2]

Is She Ready to Go?

How do you and your mother know when she is ready to go into an ALF? Basically, you can apply the same tests you did in Chapter 7 to determine whether she needs a nonmedical caregiver at home. She could be forgetting to eat or having problems taking care of herself. Tasks around the house could be slipping—spoiled food in the refrigerator and a rug that needs cleaning. Be on the lookout for even more striking indicators such as dramatic weight loss (or gain) and doctor-directed special diets. You fear it might be dangerous for her to be home alone.

Are You Prepared to Address the Four Most Important Issues?

1. Adequate finances to afford assisted living?

2. Loss of independence?

3. Loss of old friends with this move?

4. Loss of possessions required in the transition from home to assisted living?

Yet family care at home, backed up by professional nonmedical aides, is not an easy alternative. You live in California, and your parents live in Ohio. None of your siblings live in Ohio anymore either, and your parents turn down your offer to have them move to California close to you. Supervising professional care from afar is possible, and Home Instead Senior Care and other superior agencies do an excellent job caring for seniors even when family caregivers are distant. Still, you might feel less anxiety about your mother if you know that help is only a few feet away and around-the-clock.

Give Her Guidance

Under those circumstances, an ALF is certainly an option. But it is not an easy one. Even though your mother acknowledges that she has her off days in which she is forgetful or lazy, she is still proud and not yet entirely convinced of her diminished powers and that it is time to leave her longtime home. She has to come to believe on her own that an ALF is where she belongs at this stage of her life. However, while your mother will make the decision herself, that doesn't mean you can't give her guidance.

By and large, seniors have four big concerns about moving into an ALF. They worry about the financial cost, the loss of independence, the possibility that they won't have any friends, and that they will have to abandon the possessions of a lifetime.

There are answers to these concerns, of course. And it may surprise you to learn that answered correctly, you will be able to turn negatives into positives. Consider the following responses: Yes, an ALF is expensive, but you can find one that is within her means; besides, her physical and mental well-being are more important than money. Yes, she will probably have to leave many possessions behind, but she can hold on to important ones. And, no, your mother won't lose her independence. As a matter of fact, she can have as much independence in an ALF as she can handle, probably more than she now has at home, and she will likely end up with more friends nearby than she has had in a long time.

A New Experience

Your mother's concern about moving out of the four-bedroom house in which she raised her children and knows every nook and cranny is understandable. Half of ALF apartments are studios or efficiency units. The great majority of the rest have only one bedroom, with only a few two-bedroom units.[3] But point out to her that she can bring her own bed and dresser and surround herself with other lifelong possessions to make her feel at home.

Supervisors are on the premises twenty-four hours a day in case of a crisis. They will make sure your mother does not wander aimlessly from her apartment during the evening, a distressing practice on the part of some seniors with dementia.[4] Also, if your mother has trouble adjusting to life in an ALF and you are far away, you can retain an agency like Home Instead Senior Care to have a professional caregiver spend time with her through the difficult initial period.

Worth the Cost?

ALFs can be expensive. The national average ALF base rate was just over $3,000 a month in 2008, but rates vary by location and services offered, with some facilities charging $6,000 a month or more.[5] Private insurance may help with the costs, but Medicaid does not pay for ALF costs, as it eventually does for nursing home costs. We'll discuss that in greater detail in the next chapter. Still, the freedom your mother will enjoy in an ALF compared with a nursing home is probably worth the cost, if your family can afford it.

Do You Understand the Actual Costs?

- What basic services are included in the monthly fee?
- Are there services you are paying for but may not need?
- If so, can you negotiate a lower or different fee?

An ALF, moreover, can be more than supportive. It can be a life-enriching experience for your mother. Her apartment will come equipped with at least a kitchenette, if your mother wants to prepare her own meals. But she never has to cook again if she doesn't want to. She can have three healthy meals a day in a group dining room. The staff will also take care of linen and laundry and personal care, such as help with bathing, dressing, and toileting. Staff members will make certain she takes her medications, and they will arrange transportation for her when she wants to leave the premises for shopping or a visit home. Many of these services are covered in the monthly fee, but make sure to clarify in advance what is included.[6]

Health Benefits

Your mother's physical and mental health might actually rally when she moves into an ALF. Here's how to help assure that. When choosing an ALF, you will obviously make a selection based in part on costs, the physical surroundings, safety standards, licenses, and nearness to you and other family members.

But search as well for an ALF that will not be passive in its care of your mother, in other words, simply making sure that no harm comes to her. Look for an ALF with an energetic, creative staff determined to make her life better through physical exercise, brain games, and social activities.[7] Remember, too, that satisfaction with meals is a major consideration in choosing an ALF. You can make your own check of food quality by visiting for lunch or dinner.

When you investigate an ALF, find out whether it is able to cope with seniors who develop Alzheimer's or other forms of dementia, advises Grimes. What sometimes happens, he points out, is that after a few years, a resident begins to develop symptoms of dementia. The ALF tells her and her family that she has to move because they can't provide a secure environment for her. Disrupting your mother's life at that point, after she has settled in to the ALF and found a new community for herself, is heartbreaking.

Begin your search for an ALF by contacting your local Area Agency on Aging or one of the other sources listed at the end of this chapter. When you visit the several ALFs that look promising, ask the director about the facilities and structured programs they have to help keep your mother young. Look around at the residents. Do they look healthy and happy for their ages, and are they socializing? Three kinds of activity are key.

Exercise. Your mother has likely heard as much as the rest of us about the importance of physical exercise, but she may have convinced herself that the benefits are bestowed only on the young or middle-aged. She is too old to start working out, she thinks. Also, she feels foolish or vulnerable walking or practicing Tai Chi by herself. Living in an ALF with an active and well-attended physical exercise program could provide her with both the opportunity and the peer pressure she needs.

Many studies strongly suggest that physical exercise can slow down or even reverse some of the effects of aging. Strength training with machines, dumbbells, and wrist and ankle weights has proven to be a "safe and effective means by which to improve physical capabilities, prevent functional limitations, and avert the development of certain chronic diseases or their symptoms in older adults," concludes Miriam E. Nelson, Ph.D., of the Friedman School of Nutrition Science and Policy at Tufts University.[8]

Mental Benefits, Too. "The benefits of strength training include increased muscle and bone mass, muscle strength, flexibility, dynamic balance, self-confidence, and self-esteem," Nelson continues. "Strength training also helps reduce the symptoms of various chronic diseases such as arthritis, depression, type 2 diabetes, osteoporosis, sleep disorders, and heart disease, and, when combined with balance training, reduces falls."

Exercise may also have significant mental benefits. Researchers at Columbia University Medical Center discovered recently that exercise helps build a section of the brain associated with age-related memory loss.[9]

Our ability to commit material to memory probably peaks when we are in our twenties, according to widespread research. By fifty many people have observed the frequent failures of short-term memory. At seventy many seniors fear their ability to remember is sinking rapidly.

But those abilities can be rescued. In fact, recent research has shown that in the healthy aging brain, new synapses can continue to form, and nerve cells can regenerate. Nearly 90 percent of those surveyed said they believe that it is possible to improve cognitive fitness—so it's not surprising that more than 80 percent of these participants reported that they regularly took time to engage in activities that may be associated with improved cognitive health: engaging in creative projects, reading, physical activity, spending time with family and friends, doing puzzles, or playing games.[10]

Honing Recall Skills. Consequently, Country Meadows, a group of ten ALFs in Pennsylvania and Maryland, has adopted the Brain Fitness Program with impressive results, according to

Sandy Strathmeyer, director for dementia care. One happy participant was Carol, who moved to the Country Meadows ALF in Harrisburg at the age of eighty-one. She had been a busy volunteer.

Then she fractured a hip, and discouragement became a constant companion. "I was confined to my room an entire year, and I began to feel pretty worthless," she said. "I felt that I wasn't measuring up because I was not doing anything positive other than trying to get better." Carol noticed something else: the reading that she always enjoyed was becoming much more of a challenge.

So she enrolled in the care community's Brain Fitness Program. Along with other residents, she visited a computer lab an hour a day for a total of forty sessions over eight weeks. The program provided Carol a boost in a number of ways. "I'm much more aware of things I hear on the TV and radio, and while talking to people," she said. "And I'm more inclined to try to recall that information."[11]

Late-Life Surge

Other evidence supports the case for brain exercise. Researchers at the University of New South Wales in Sydney, Australia, found that individuals with high brain reserve, that is, those who have benefited from high levels of education, complexity in their occupations, and mentally stimulating pursuits off the job, have 46 percent less risk of dementia than those with low brain reserve. Good news for the elderly is that the study concluded that even a late-life surge in mental activity can stave off the effects of this terrible disease.[12]

Your mother may have had a busy social calendar earlier in her life, one full of dinner parties and church outings, bridge games and movies that filled her evenings. Anticipating and planning those get-togethers, the brisk conversation and laughter that accompanied them, including the gossip, bolstered her naturally cheerful, optimistic temperament and kept her looking forward to the next evening, the next week. But as her health declined, she has stayed home more and more evenings, relying on television rather than real people to kill the hours before she could fall asleep.

Enterprising managers of ALFs are doing their best to get their residents back into that energizing social swing. Two of the most effective in recent years are Tim Cook, Jr., former general manager of the Bridge at Life Care Center in Columbia, Tennessee, and Eric Dobner, activities director at Narrows Glen in Tacoma, Washington.[13]

Cook thinks of his ALF residents as content vacationers on a cruise ship that never reaches port. "And that's the way it needs to be," Cook said. "Once you step on board, there should be something for you every hour of the day. I've had a lot of residents tell me they feel like they're on vacation."[14]

Home Environment

Like many ALF managers, Cook understands the need for residents to have access to meaningful schedules after dinner as well as during the day—particularly events that mirror the home environment many left behind. Scheduling diversions that go into the evening hours is a challenge. Many residents tire easily, and there are fewer staff members available to help.

But Cook uses his imagination and available resources. For example, the receptionist at Cook's seventy-unit facility is a ballroom dancer who has competed professionally. So Cook asked her to organize ballroom dancing for the residents twice a month. Theme nights also are popular. "If we're having a Mexican dinner, we'll decorate and bring in a mariachi band," Cook said.[15]

An ALF manager can't force a resident to participate in activities, but gentle persuasion, persistent reminders, and customized activities help ensure that 75 to 90 percent of their residents take part in some events.

"Part of my job and that of my assistant is to contact as many residents as possible about what's going on," said Dobner of the Tacoma facility. "Sometimes we'll make phone calls to residents. Monthly calendars and weekly activity sheets also help."[16]

"A lady who moved into our facility is very fun and social with a great sense of humor," observed Dobner. "But she wouldn't come out of her apartment. What first got her out was our Friday morning coffeehouse outings. She loves movies, so then she started coming out at night for those. She's doing great now."

Engaging the Resident

Finding a resident's interest is often the key to motivating that individual to participate in an activity. "We've had trouble getting one resident to interact with others because she doesn't feel

---

Does the Assisted Living Facility Offer . . .

- proximity to family and friends?
- dining services?
- housekeeping and laundry services?
- assistance with medications?
- transportation for shopping and medical appointments?
- exercise and fitness facilities and classes?
- an in-house pharmacy with prices comparable to market prices?
- programs to stimulate the brain?
- social programs?
- personalized activities in which your senior could engage?
- all of the above included in the monthly fee?

like she needs to be here. We found out she was a tour guide and has videos of many of her trips. So beginning in January we've asked her to host getaway nights where she will narrate a trip to a different location and show her videos. We're all excited about starting that," said former Tennessee facility manager Cook.

A resident in the early stages of dementia had seldom left the house in a decade, recalled Cook. "When she got here, it was only a week before she flourished," he added. "When we had our senior prom, our receptionist was dancing, and this resident was trying to mimic her every move. It brought her son to tears. He couldn't say enough about how much better she was doing. Her family is here all the time now because she's more energetic and lively and fun to be around. We couldn't imagine her any other way."[17]

The Next Step

So after a hesitant beginning, your mother may well come to love her new community and friends at her ALF. Some seniors live out the rest of their lives contentedly in ALFs. But unfortunately it often happens that after a year or two of improvement, they begin to decline to a level that makes life in an ALF difficult. At that point, they may be better off in a skilled nursing home, which we will discuss in the next chapter.

Assisted Living Facilities

Assisted living provides relatively independent seniors with assistance and limited health care services in a homelike atmosphere. Assisted living services include twenty-four-hour protective oversight, food, shelter, and a range of services that promote the quality of life of the individual.

Advantages
- Minimize the need to relocate
- Accommodate individual residents' changing needs and preferences
- Maximize residents' dignity, autonomy, privacy, independence, choice, and safety
- Encourage family and community involvement

Disadvantages
- Depression may be triggered by the loss of independence when older people move to assisted living facilities.
- Pharmacies affiliated with assisted living facilities will often charge residents more for prescriptions than an independent pharmacy would.
- The average resident stays only two years.

Choose This Option If
- Senior is beginning to need help with the basic activities of daily living (bathing, dressing, grooming, walking, managing medications, toileting, and eating)

Average Annual Cost
- The national average, private-pay monthly base rate for an individual residing in an assisted living community is $2,969, or $35,628 annually.

Resources Available

- Assisted Living Federation of America, alfa.org
- Consumer Consortium on Assisted Living, ccal.org
- HelpGuide.org's assisted living website, helpguide.org/elder/assisted_living_facilities.htm
- National Center for Assisted Living, ncal.org/about/facility.cfm
- Total Living Choices, tlchoices.com

Issues You Should Be Aware Of

- While assisted living facilities are residential in character, there is no standard blueprint because consumers' preferences and needs vary so greatly.

When It Is Time to Move On

- Senior is dependent on twenty-four-hour skilled care provided by licensed nurses
- Senior has serious medical condition that requires specialized care

11

Skilled Nursing Homes

We began this book reflecting on the fact that only a few decades ago there were only two choices for adult children seeking to protect their parents in their declining years. The children could bring frail parents into their own homes, or they could send them to nursing homes. Many nursing homes were run by religious groups and other people of goodwill who lovingly cared for the elderly in their final years as best they could.

But the financial resources of nursing homes were generally limited. Their staffs were overworked, so their elderly residents were often ignored. The facilities were neglected, often rundown. Society's mental picture of a nursing home was that of a gloomy waiting station at the edge of the graveyard.

Nursing homes, much better financed now, by and large have changed dramatically over the years. In the past two decades a revolutionary concept called the Eden Alternative has helped transform some nursing homes from warehouses for the elderly into places where seniors are encouraged to express their full humanity. There is no standardized routine, and the nursing homes operate independently. Residents and staff create their own culture as they take care of dogs, raise birds, grow flowers, cook, and generally devote themselves to having fun.

An Important Role

For a reasonably healthy senior, a nursing home still is probably not the right choice. But for the senior who truly needs skilled medical care and intense supervision, it may be exactly the best place to live. Many of the best are staffed with teams of well-trained professional registered and practical nurses as well as certified nursing assistants. In case of an emergency, physicians and psychiatrists are close at hand to deal with medical crises, which should give you greater peace of mind.

So nursing homes continue to have a very important place on the spectrum of care for the elderly. The number of nursing home facilities in the United States was around 16,000 in 2004 with 1.7 million beds and 1.5 million residents.[1]

The federal and state governments make an effort to uphold standards through inspections of nursing homes, monitoring such things as the nutrition and medication of residents as well as their treatment by the staff. The industry still has problems. Despite the great improvement in nursing homes overall, 17 percent of nursing homes surveyed in 2007 were cited for dangerous deficiencies in practices or facilities, which had caused actual harm or placed residents in immediate jeopardy.[2]

Creativity Brings Improvements

Architects design some of the best nursing homes to look like traditional homes. They are brightly and sometimes elaborately decorated and offer residents a great variety of activities to keep

Choose the Right Nursing Home

- Visit, observe, ask, and try.
- Check ratio of nurses and nursing assistants to residents.
- Determine staff tenure and turnover.
- Ask about physician availability: full-time or part-time?
- How close is the closest hospital?
- Review the most recent oversight-agency survey.
- Look for activities offered by the facility.
- Check the food by inviting yourself to meals.
- Check exercise and entertainment offerings.
- Determine if speech and physical therapy services are offered.
- Consider proximity to family.
- Understand the cost and financing options.

their minds and bodies active: arts and crafts classes, gardening, yoga, and exercise. Some nursing homes provide exercise rooms and workout equipment. Musicians and artists who work or live near nursing homes volunteer to entertain the residents. School children often visit as well, and many nursing homes now encourage the staff to bring in their pets to cheer up the residents. Most nursing homes offer a high level of supervision and safety as well.

Senior Pets for Seniors

Are pets good for seniors? The answer is a qualified "yes." But like every step along the senior care continuum, there are some very important things to consider as you weigh whether it makes sense to bring a new animal home.

Barb Cathey is the founder and president of Pets for Seniors. Her organization matches cats and dogs from shelters and foster pet groups with senior citizens. She started her work after seeing a wonderful "senior" dog put to sleep for lack of an owner. A senior couple had spent time playing with the dog but then left the shelter with a puppy instead. When they returned the puppy a week later because it was too much of a handful for them, they asked about the "senior" dog, but it was too late.

Cathey believes that putting senior citizens and senior pets together makes a lot of sense. When a senior comes to her looking for a pet, "compatibility" is her guide. In general, she observes that a "senior" pet tends to be well trained and calmer, and calmness is critical for most seniors who thrive on the companionship but can do without the travails of puppyhood or a hyperactive pet.

Cathey also stresses compatibility when it comes to the planning. A young dog has a much higher chance of outliving its owner—a senior dog reduces this age incompatibility. You want to see that the senior cares about what happens to the animal, too. Another concern might be a senior who is contemplating entering an assisted living facility; he or she will likely be limited in his or her pet choices. When they do allow pets, Cathey notes, assisted living facilities limit the weight of the pet to fifteen pounds, so a big dog is out of the question. Nursing homes don't allow residents to keep their own pets. Cathey provides a checklist for determining compatibility:

- How well behaved is the dog on a walk? Is it calm? Does it sit to have a leash put on?
- Is the animal aggressive around food or toys?
- Is the dog good with cats? Is the cat good with dogs?
- Does the pet like to sit on laps, especially important for many seniors?

These issues aside, Cathey has seen pets change seniors' lives. "The animals become their family," she says, and remembers one woman who in two weeks went from being depressed to engagement in life after receiving a cat about whom she spoke nonstop. Pet companions can also widen a senior's world by taking them out in the world.

For those who can't adopt or don't want to, animals can still make a huge difference in a senior's quality of life. There are a number of organizations like Pets on Wheels, Inc. (petsonwheels .org) and Therapy Dogs International (tdi-dog.org) that arrange for pet visitation of seniors in nursing homes and assisted living communities across the country. When assessing an assisted living community or a nursing home, ask whether it keeps house pets that all residents can befriend.

No matter how pleasant the surroundings and how good the care, a nursing home, nonetheless, is a place that very few seniors look forward to going to, and for understandable reasons. Some people go to nursing homes temporarily to recuperate from a broken hip, perhaps, or a stroke, and then return home or to another agreeable setting.

But once admitted, many nursing home residents will live out the rest of their lives there, and most are likely aware of that, at least at some level of consciousness. Even in the best nursing homes, they are in the constant company of terminally sick people like themselves, many of them suffering from dementia, who are ever-present reminders of mortality.

Around-the-Clock Care

Why then does a senior enter a nursing home? In some cases the senior initiates the decision to go to a nursing home. But often it is the family that begins the process. The loved one is no longer the clearheaded and relatively fit senior who made the independent decision to buy a retirement home or go into assisted living. The senior for whom a nursing home is an option is generally quite sick, his or her mental awareness sharply limited. Incontinence and dementia are among the major reasons people are admitted to nursing homes.

Neither the family nor the professional caregivers can manage him or her at home any longer, a reality that may well be lost on the senior. She is now so fragile she needs a caregiver around the clock. She may no longer be able to eat unassisted, use the toilet, or get out of bed. Or he might wander away if he isn't constantly supervised, and the family or other caregiver can no longer cope with the erratic behavior that puts his life in danger.

"A lot of people are living on the edge at home," says Mary Fran Fleming, an administrator at the Hebrew Home at Riverdale, New York, one of the nation's premiere nursing homes.

"Their medical conditions are barely stable, and once they start fluctuating into instability, the nursing home is an option. This might be a woman with low blood pressure who suddenly faints and is taken to an emergency room. Another common reason for sending someone to a nursing home is dementia, which could be Alzheimer's or some lesser form of cognitive impairment. Of our 868 residents, 58 percent suffer from dementia."

Finding the Appropriate Home

How do you find the appropriate nursing home for your mother? We are going to assume in this example that it is your mother who is in need, rather than your father, because in a typical nursing home, the majority of the population is female. You might be surprised to learn that your mother has already given the matter

Phyllis Gets a Life

When Phyllis came to the nursing home with heart problems at the age of seventy-three, she left behind an unhappy life she didn't like to talk about. But whatever those troubles were, they certainly didn't drag her down at the nursing home. Five days a week Phyllis tutored nearby high school students in English and math; one Sunday a month she mentored teenagers in a literacy program. She served as a volunteer at the nursing home's polling place on Election Day. Classes in painting, tiling, beading, and ceramics took up much of the rest of her time. Finally, with the encouragement of the nursing home's staff, Phyllis started taking classes on social work at a local college. "These have been some of the happiest and most productive days of my life," she told fellow residents during a slide show on her nursing home career. She then rushed off to finish her homework.

some thought because she already has friends in various nursing homes and wants to be with them. Certainly your mother should have a vote in the choice. But help her conduct a scientific search.

Start by consulting with the federally sponsored website at medicare.gov/nhcompare. It will list the nursing homes in your area and evaluate them according to a number of quality measures.

But Fleming points out that you may have to dig below the raw data offered in those evaluations. For example, one measure of quality is the "wound care rate," which means the incidence of pressure ulcers, also known as bedsores. "A good nursing home should not have any patients who acquire bedsores while under their care," says Fleming, "however, a good nursing home could have a special wound care center, which means it is taking in bedsore problems from other health care facilities." Ask the nursing home to explain any poor grades in the website evaluations.

Visit the Finalists

Narrow your choices to three or four nursing homes and then visit them. Don't be deceived by the look of the physical plant, advises Larry Minnix, chief executive of the American Association of Homes and Services for the Aging. "In some of the older homes, the buildings don't look very nice," he says. "But the service is really good because the staff cares about the residents. In fact, a lot of times nursing homes in small towns, where everybody knows each other, are better than nursing homes in big cities, because in the small town, the staff is taking care of people who used to be their schoolteachers."

It is hard for a visitor to determine the quality of the staff. But ask what kind of physician coverage the home has. Is the physician part-time or full-time? What are the difficulties in getting the physician to come, such as distance from the home, in case of an emergency? How close is an acute care hospital in case of a major emergency? What are ambulance service arrangements?

Do you smell an unpleasant odor? That is likely the result of patients sitting in their urine for long periods, which indicates that the staff is not caring for them as soon as the accident occurs. Ask the nursing home administrator to explain the smell. As you tour the nursing home, look for signs of poor housekeeping and sanitation.

Observe the residents that you meet in the hallways and dining room and elsewhere. Do they seem to be well cared for and reasonably content? Don't expect to see a lot of easy social inter-

Sadie Takes a Flight

It wasn't until Sadie entered a nursing home that she realized she had the spirit and stamina to be a world traveler. Before Sadie entered the Hebrew Home at Riverdale, New York, she had never ventured overseas. Indeed, her devoted son, who visited her in the nursing home every Sunday, considered her so fragile that he wouldn't even take her off campus for dinner. Then an executive of the nursing home decided he wanted to tour Israel and thought it would be a good idea to bring along ten nursing home residents as well. "Just because you're old doesn't mean you can't have a dream," the executive explained to the residents. Sadie, about to turn ninety, signed up for the trip. She loved it and returned to the United States and the home energized. "If I can go to Israel, I can go to a restaurant," she mildly scolded her overprotective son. She also persuaded him to take her along to her granddaughter's college graduation in Washington, D.C.

action among residents, however. Keep in mind that generally residents of a nursing home have been admitted because they are in considerable physical or mental distress. Your mother will be able to make friends among staff and fellow residents, and perhaps even find love. But many residents are locked inside themselves, prisoners of their dementia.

How Are Behavioral Problems Managed?

Ask the nursing home administrator if residents with advanced Alzheimer's or other severe dementia are separated from other residents in special sections of the home. Such segregation might sound cruel. But consider this: Sadly, residents with severe dementia are often unable to control themselves and sometimes roam the hallways and can even become violent. If a woman in such a condition wanders into your mother's room, rummages through her closet, and turns the contents of her bureau upside down, your mother will be understandably terrified.

The separation is often best also for the residents suffering from severe dementia. Many nursing homes provide them with special care in their own units, where the environment is geared to their level of understanding and ability to cope. The TV does not play noisy game shows but rather soothing concerts or sounds of ocean waves breaking on shore.

Look at Ratios of Nurses to Residents

Homes are required to post on the wall for visitors to see the ratio of residents to nurses and nursing assistants. "Here are the most important questions you can ask about staffing," suggests Minnix. "How many hours of nursing care do you provide per resident per twenty-four hours? What is your staff turnover? How many people have been working here for five years, ten years, or longer?" Also ask to see the latest survey conducted by the state regulatory agency, which will list any deficiencies, such as errors in medications and falls by residents. If there are no negatives on the survey, that's a good sign.

Look on the walls also for postings of activities, such as concerts, painting classes, ceramics, and card clubs. Ask about the wellness program and what provisions the home has for other physical exercise. Does the nursing home offer speech therapy and dental care and any special services your mother might need, such as physical therapy for recovering from a broken limb? Some nursing homes are equipped to handle kidney dialysis and have ventilators to assist breathing.

Geography Is Key

Many nursing homes still have religious affiliations, and although they are not allowed to discriminate in admissions on that basis, if your mother has spent her entire life in one denomination, she might feel out of place in a home managed by another.

Geography is extremely important. Find a nursing home that is not prohibitively far away from Mom's traditional home and family and, ideally, is well served by public transportation. Sad to say, as much as they love your mother, family and friends find visiting a nursing home depressing and often avoid the trip. Don't give them any additional excuses to stay away. The staff notices when residents have visitors, who will keep track of whether the room is unkempt or your mother's wishes are ignored. Visitors can make the staff more attentive.

"The most important thing that any family member can do is stay involved, " says Dr. Keren Brown-Wilson, a professor in the Institute on Aging at Portland State University and the president of the Jessie F. Richardson Foundation, a charitable organization that works with indigent elders. "That means participating regularly in what's going on in that person's life. If you come in from out of town one time and there's a mess in your mother's room, it may or may not be a problem. If you consistently go every Sunday, and it's always a mess, you know there's a problem."

Financing a Stay

Financing a stay in a nursing home is almost always complicated and inevitably expensive. The high cost is justifiable. Nursing homes require an extraordinary number of trained staff members to take care of frail people who can do little for themselves. Many of the residents are incapable of eating, bathing, going to the toilet, changing clothes, or moving from their rooms to elsewhere in the home without help.

The average cost of a private room in a nursing home in 2008 was $212 a day, or $77,380 a year; the average cost of a semiprivate room was $191 a day, or $69,715 a year. There are considerable cost differences by region, however, so ask the nursing homes you are considering about their rates.[3]

It's easy to see why the savings of many seniors are wiped out by nursing home stays. We hope this observation will underscore for you the value and importance of purchasing long-term care insurance. Once your loved ones have reached the stage at which going into a nursing home is imminent, it is too late to think about buying such insurance for them. But in Chapter 17, we will talk about financing care and stress the importance of buying long-term care insurance early on, for your parents—and for yourself.

Getting Help

Gaining admission to the first choice nursing home for your mother is not always easy. Waiting lists can be long. Perhaps the simplest method of getting in and working out a financial arrangement with a nursing home is if your mother is first admitted to a Medicare-accredited hospital for any of a variety of reasons. Perhaps she has fainting spells or has fractured a limb or needs surgery. We will assume your mother is covered by Medicare or a Medicare Advantage program, as almost everyone over the age of sixty-five is.

From Hospital to Nursing Home

Medicare will pay most of her bills while she is in the hospital. Medicare's reimbursement to the hospital is a fixed amount, what Medicare calls a "prospective payment," but the hospital may consider the amount to be too low. Consequently, the hospital may be eager to discharge her as soon as her condition is stable. But before they can discharge her, laws require that they find a safe place to send her. You are no longer able to care for her at home, so you must be a strong advocate at the hospital for getting her into her nursing home of first choice.

In the nursing home, Medicare may pay for care up to a maximum of 100 days.[4] To qualify for any Medicare-paid nursing home benefit, your mother must have spent three nights in the hospital and must enter the nursing home within thirty days for rehabilitation for the same condition treated in the hospital. If all those conditions are met, Medicare fully covers the first twenty days of her care and partially for up to the next eighty days.[5]

Note that Medicare's definition of rehab requires that your mother's therapy continues to produce results, such as improved healing, strength, coordination, and flexibility. Once your mother stops improving, Medicare stops paying, even if it's been less than twenty days.

What to Do When Medicare Stops Paying

Families are often shocked and angry when they realize that Medicare will no longer pay, even though Mom may still need a high level of care and attention. Medicare only covers short-term care, and then only when it is measurably rehabilitative.

Before admission, the nursing home will ask how your mother intends to pay once Medicare payments end. Long-term insurance will pay for part of it, and a deluxe policy might pay for all of her care for a long time. Otherwise, nursing homes will ask for her financial statements, and it will require her to personally pay for care and services, which may require spending her savings as well as her income. If she has assets of $70,000 when she enters the nursing home, say, chances are they will be exhausted within a year. That drawdown may come as a blow to your family and its expectations. But it is not unreasonable. In exchange, most homes will take care of your mother for as long as she lives and help her apply for Medicaid, assuming the nursing home participates in the state-run welfare program. Not all nursing homes take Medicaid reimbursements, so if you think your mother will need financial assistance, check with the nursing home before your mother is admitted.

Medicaid Will Take Over

When your mother has used or sold all of her assets, including her home, to pay for her care, Medicaid will begin to pay the nursing home on her behalf. Medicaid regulations vary greatly from state to state, however, so be certain that you understand your state's rules. Medicaid prohibits your mother from intentionally impoverishing herself—by giving her house and other financial assets to you and the rest of the family, for example—in order to qualify. Some states look back through her financial records for the five years before she applied for Medicaid.

In general, Medicaid reimburses the nursing home at a lower rate than private patients pay, so the nursing home wants your mother to keep paying as a private patient for as long as possible. Moreover, your mother cannot qualify for Medicaid until she, or more likely you, can demonstrate that she is truly indigent. The regulations that govern these decisions vary by state. (The limit is higher if there is a spouse who is still living independently.) Once your mother has qualified for Medicaid, the monthly payments she receives from Social Security or a pension must be paid toward her cost of care, with Medicaid only making up the difference.

Looking over the passages we have just written, we recognize how difficult and depressing we have made the nursing home experience seem. That presentation will perhaps add to your feelings of guilt about placing your mother there. It seems like a betrayal of the hope of having a loved one die peaceably in her own bed, fully conscious of being surrounded by her devoted family.

You've Done Your Best

That ideal passing away happens sometimes, but mostly it doesn't. The end of life is more often confused and muddled, the precise time unexpected. You should not feel guilty because you couldn't make it tidy or serene. By finding the best nursing home, visiting your mother often, and encouraging other family and friends to do the same, you will be doing your best to make her final months as rich and comfortable as you can. The best you can do is see to it that she has the right care at every step along the way throughout the entire process. In modern parlance, you will help her achieve a peaceful closure.

In the next chapter, we will talk about hospice care, which is by and large a more tranquil experience for both the failing senior and the family.

Nursing Homes

Also known as a skilled nursing facility, or SNF, this option offers registered nurses who help provide twenty-four-hour care to people who can no longer care for themselves due to physical, emotional, or mental conditions. Most nursing homes have two basic types of services: skilled medical care (provided by a nurse or doctor) and custodial care (maintenance care that includes assistance with the activities of daily living).

Advantages
- Around-the-clock care
- Provides a sense of community
- Not as risky as they once were; now undergo evaluations by Medicare

Disadvantages
- Can be very expensive
- Loneliness can be an issue
- Individual's freedom and independence may be sacrificed

Choose This Option If
- Senior cannot take care of themselves because of physical, emotional, or mental problems
- Senior might wander away if unsupervised
- Senior has been recommended for a nursing home by a physician

Average Annual Cost
- The national average daily rate for a private room in a nursing home is $212, or $77,380 annually

Resources Available

- American Association of Homes and Services for the Aging, aahsa.org
- National Citizen's Coalition for Nursing Home Reform, nccnhr.org
- Nursing Home Compare, medicare.gov/nhcompare

Issues You Should Be Aware Of

As you tour a nursing home facility, consider these areas:

- Safety
- Livability
- Nutrition

When It Is Time to Move On

- Physician recommendation

12

Hospice Care

There may come a time in the final stages of your loved one's life that she is ill and no longer responds to medical care, or where medical intervention would cause more suffering than could be justified by any improvement in her condition. Physicians attending her believe that she is in irreversible decline and likely has no more than six months to live. People can arrive at this disheartening juncture in any of the homes or settings we have described so far.

Commonly one reaches this point after a long stay in a nursing home. But it could happen in a hospital or while she is under the direct care of you and other family members, or even while she is living independently.

At this point it would be wise to think about hospice care. Hospice is very much a part of the care process, a continuation of what you have been doing all along—assuring that your loved one gets the best care possible for whatever her stage of life and health.

What Is Hospice?

Probably no form of senior care is as little understood as hospice. People often have misconceptions about it and almost always questions. Is it a building, like a hospital? Who are the professionals who will take care of my mother in hospice care? How much, or how little, will they do for her? If nursing home costs have impoverished her, how will she, or we, pay for hospice care? What role does the family play in hospice care?

Hospice care is sometimes thought of as a synonym for palliative care. That's not too far wrong, but hospice care is really a particular kind of palliative care. Palliative care is a form of treatment that does not attempt to cure the patient's underlying disease. Rather it focuses on alleviating the symptoms of the disease, especially reducing the pain. People of any age can undergo palliative care, among them children suffering from cancer.

Hospice Care and Palliative Care: What's the Difference?

- Palliative care is designed to alleviate symptoms, especially reducing pain.
- People of any age can receive palliative care, including those who simultaneously receive healing care.
- Hospice is a particular kind of palliative care, limited to those who are judged by medical professionals to be at the end of life but are still in need of pain relief and comfort.

Eliminating Pain

Palliative care does not preclude other medical care. It is possible, for example, to have one team of doctors alleviating the pain of a child with leukemia, in other words, practicing palliative care, while other specialists focus on curing the child's disease.

In contrast, hospice care is limited to those who are judged by medical professionals to be at the end of their lives, generally, but not exclusively, the elderly. The purpose, as with other forms of palliative care, is to eliminate or at least control pain and suffering. The promise to the individual who is placed in hospice care is that she will be able to spend her final weeks and days with as much dignity and as little pain as possible. Hospice care professionals assist the patient with the emotional and spiritual aspects of death as well.[1]

No Aggressive Treatments

Under hospice, aggressive treatments—those aimed at treating an illness—are not done. Indeed, the Medicare rules governing hospice care prohibit payment for treatments aimed at prolonging life, rather than simply making life more endurable.[2]

Before describing hospice further, let's mention two rules that protect hospice patients.

▪ No one can be forced into hospice care against her will; she must sign a consent form.[3] Your mother might not be mentally alert enough to sign such a form at the time hospice becomes an option, which underscores why it is important for everyone, not just your parents, to fill out an advance directive (living will) while they are in good mental health and able to clarify their wishes under such circumstances. In that document, your mother would have given instructions like the following: "If my death from a terminal condition is imminent and even if life-sustaining procedures were to be used, there is no reasonable expectation of my recovery, I direct my life not be extended by life-sustaining procedures." She would also have specified whether she wanted painkillers. (See Chapter 3.)

▪ Nor is the decision to go into hospice care irrevocable, as is commonly believed, since the patient or representative retains the right to cease hospice care at any time.[4] For instance, your mother might decide to leave the hospice program to take part instead in an experimental treatment.

A patient may have reached the stage at which she is ready for hospice care when she makes repeated trips to the emergency room and is treated but doesn't bounce back. Perhaps she has also become emotionally withdrawn, sleeps more, or has more and more difficulty understanding conversations, or where she is presently, or even recognizing you. She may be in increasing pain and have more and more trouble breathing.

It is up to medical professionals, of course, not loved ones, to determine that no treatment will change the course of a debilitat-

A Simple, Wooded Place

Frederick, eighty-six and a retired psychiatrist, was familiar with all the options medicine has to offer those who appear to be at the end of life. Still, he chose the simplest, least clinical alternative. Suffering from leukemia, he elected to spend his final months as simply as possible, at a very small residential hospice in a peaceful wooded town in upstate New York. Family members visited Frederick in his bedroom and chatted quietly with volunteers in the comfortable, unpretentious living room. One of the volunteers had brought along her dog, which added to the homelike ambience. A nurse visited, noted that Frederick's breathing was labored, and wanted to give him oxygen. Frederick's daughter, an emergency room physician, persuaded her not to do so. Like others in his condition, Frederick's daughter said, her father would simply rip the oxygen mask off. All he wanted in the end was painkillers. The nurse respected his wishes.

ing disease. But it may well be up to you to inform your mother of the doctors' evaluation and to help her with decisions about hospice care. How do you do that? Clearly, it is one of the most difficult conversations, perhaps the most difficult, of your life.

We have no glib answers about how to conduct that excruciating conversation. To guide you, it can help to talk to other family and friends who know your mother well and know how she feels about her life. We encourage you to take into account your senior's religious beliefs—perhaps engage your pastor, rabbi, or other spiritual counselor to help you through this conversation. We will talk more about this difficult decision and its repercussions later in the chapter.

At its best, hospice care can be an ennobling experience, especially if your mother expressed her wishes freely and coura-

Choosing Hospice Care: What to Look For

Here are some other things to look for when assessing the suitability of a hospice provider for your loved one:

General Information
- Is the hospice licensed, certified, or accredited? If so, for what types of services?
- Is the agency bonded (insured against liability)?
- Are services provided at home or in a facility?

What Types of Services Are Offered?
- Emergency care or arranging for hospitalization
- Physical therapy
- Massage therapy
- Ventilator care
- Home-delivered meals

What Types of Service Providers Are Available—and Can You Get References on Them?
- Psychologist
- Therapist/counselor
- Spiritual advisor
- Volunteer

How Will Your Loved One's Individual Care Needs Be Met?
- Is a written statement provided regarding eligibility, payment, and staff training?
- Is the individual care plan done in consultation with your loved one's physician?

- Is there a grievance procedure in case I, as the caregiver, disagree with the way care is delivered?
- Will I, as the caregiver, have contact with a hospice supervisor?

Source: CareGuide@Home, "Living Alternatives: Hospice Checklist," careguideathome.com/modules.php?op=modload&name=CG _Resources&file=article&sid=1068 (accessed January 28, 2009).

geously at a time when she could reflect rationally on her life, its meaning, and how it should end. You are now going to guide her through the final weeks or months, comforting her as her assured and devoted companion on the path she planned.

This is a chance to help her reconcile with any family members or friends who have drifted away over the years. It is also your chance to sustain her through her final wishes and duties. As a colleague of ours who lost his wife to cancer expressed the fulfillment of being at her side throughout hospice care put the responsibility, "It is one of the highest privileges to help someone in the last weeks or days of her life."

Hospice: Then and Now

Hospice care is a relatively new regimen and still developing. Although there are some antecedents going back hundreds of years, the first modern hospice (the word is derived from the same linguistic root as is "hospitality"), St. Christopher's Hospice of southeast London, England, was founded in 1967. In the 1970s, the hospice movement began growing in the United States, a trend that has since gained almost continual momentum.[5] For

Some Facts About Hospice Care

- There are no aggressive interventions to achieve recovery from sickness or disease; therefore, there is no aggressive radiation or chemotherapy and no transfusions.
- Pain control and comfort are the primary objectives.
- A decision to enter hospice care is reversible.
- Most health insurance companies cover hospice care expenses.
- Medicare covers hospice care expenses.[6]
- 90 percent of hospice care is delivered in homes, although it can also be provided in hospitals, nursing homes, and even dedicated hospice houses.
- A hospice team typically consists of a hospice physician, nurses, home health aide, social worker, chaplain, and volunteers who can help the family with housework and meals.

instance, the number of patients receiving hospice care increased nationally by nearly two-thirds from 2000 to 2005.[7]

Hospice care can be administered in a variety of settings. Nursing homes frequently offer hospice care, as do many hospitals.[8] Around the country, hundreds of residences or hospice houses that look much like family homes care for half a dozen or more patients. Some patients invent their own hospice care. When told at the age of seventy-one she was dying of a fast-spreading cancer, a society woman, who had a lot of money and taste, spent her several months of hospice care in a suite at one of New York City's best and most expensive hotels.

But most hospice patients are cared for in their own homes.[9] There they are visited by hospice care teams that could consist of a hospice physician, nurses, home health aides, social workers, chaplains, trained volunteers, and therapists. Help, although not all of the specialists named, is available twenty-four hours a day, seven days a week.[10]

Let's say something happens to your mom at 2 A.M. "The family calls, and there is a nurse to assess whether a nurse is to go to the home or if it's an urgent situation and 911 should be called," said Linda Gaetani, executive director of Denver VistaCare, the local branch of a national hospice organization that serves about 5,000 patients a day in fourteen states.

"The point being that we're available as a resource always. We also help families resolve issues during this time of hospice. Perhaps the family needs help contacting incarcerated family members. Or we get in touch with an individual's child serving in the military to get them home to see Mom and Dad for the last time."

We hope you will investigate the alternatives for hospice care in your area long before the need is urgent, for when you are told that your mother is ready for hospice care immediately, you are likely to be thrown into an emotional state that is not ideal for asking the questions that you have to put to hospice care agencies. You'll find a list of these important questions in the "Choosing Hospice Care" checklist and other important issues discussed elsewhere in this chapter.

Medicare Will Pay

Fortunately, Medicare covers most of the costs of care provided by an accredited hospice agency, whether the care is delivered at home or in a hospital or other setting. Indeed, Medicare not only supports hospice care, the program actively encourages it, for good and simple reasons. Hospice care saves Medicare, and ultimately taxpayers, considerable amounts of money because it replaces very expensive procedures, such as surgery and innovative drugs, that might extend your mother's life but will probably not cure her illness and will not necessarily improve the quality of her final weeks.[11]

The Medicare hospice benefit pays nearly all the expenses of doctor and nursing care; medical equipment and supplies; pain-killers and other drugs to control symptoms; short-term hospital treatments (for issues such as pain management); hospice aides, homemakers, and social workers; and grief support for you and your family.[12]

Understand, however, this important limitation of the Medicare hospice benefit: once your mother chooses this path—which she'll do by signing an official statement—she waives all other rights to Medicare payments for services relating to her terminal illness and any related medical conditions. That said, benefits not related to her terminal illness will still be covered.[13]

Coming to Terms

Accepting hospice care is obviously an excruciating decision for your mother—and for you. This is a turning point. Up until now all of your efforts have been directed at preserving and, when possible, enhancing her life. Now she and you are planning how it will end. Under the best circumstances, you would not be her only advisor on whether hospice is the correct choice. Your siblings and other family members will be brought into the discussion as well so that your mother can get the broadest range of advice.

Will you feel guilty about advising her to accept hospice care? Will you berate yourself for not searching for one more possible remedy for your mother's illness, some unproven, unorthodox regimen? If you are continuously anguished about your role in advising her to accept hospice, you might want to seek spiritual or psychiatric guidance, or both.

Recognize also an important escape hatch that should bring you some peace of mind. Even after your mother enters hospice care, she can rethink her decision and drop out of the program. If she does so, she will end up reverting to ordinary Medicare coverage with no hospice benefits.[14]

Choosing a Hospice Provider

Let's assume that you plan to have your mother's hospice care at her home or yours. Start your search for a hospice agency by asking your mother's physician for recommendations. Other helpful sources are geriatric care managers and such Internet websites as About.com (see the end of the chapter for a more complete list of sources). Also call the National Hospice and Palliative Care Organization HelpLine at 800-658-8898.

Like Picking a Friend

Choosing a hospice provider is as much about developing a relationship as it is about the services. Generally, hospice providers offer the same services at roughly the same level of competence. But, in the end, these are the people who will spend the final days and hours with someone you love deeply. You must be comfortable with their personalities, and—even more important—your mother needs to be comfortable. The hospice period is as much about communication and encouragement as it about administering drugs for pain.

Ask for Specifics

Don't hesitate to ask the hospice agency to tell you precisely what services it offers and at what times of the day and days of the week. Many family caregivers are under the impression that the hospice agency will take the entire burden off the family's shoulders. That is not generally the case.[15]

Help for the Family

Caregivers are sometimes stunned by the responsibilities that are left to them. A nurse might come once a day to administer medications, but the rest of the treatments might be left to the family. Hospice care patients commonly receive a confusing cluster of drugs, including morphine or other painkillers, as well as antianxiety and antihallucinatory medications. Moreover, the dosages change over time. Administering powerful drugs and knowing when to do so can be intimidating for inexperienced laypeople. Don't hesitate to call the hospice agency when you are in doubt, advises VistaCare's Linda Gaetani.

Help with Housework. Volunteers from the agency will likely help you with housework and stay with your mother while you run errands. Even if you don't have errands to run, you need time out of the house and away from the emotional strain of taking care of a loved one at the end of her life. Don't be afraid to ask siblings and friends to take turns staying with your mother. Your religious or academic community may be willing to send someone to help as well.[16]

You might want to supplement the hospice volunteers' care with that of an at-home care service, medical or nonmedical. If you think that you won't be able to care for your mother at home even with hospice and other professional help, you have the alternative of placing her in a fine hospice residence. The same

---

Vital Volunteers

A key component of hospice care is the service of volunteers, those who give their time free of charge to comforting people at the end of their lives, wherever they may be, in private homes, hospitals, hospice residences, or nursing homes. Medicare requires that at least 5 percent of the time devoted to a client's care be provided by volunteers, but the volunteers' share is often much greater than that.

Among the most active volunteer groups is the Hospice Volunteers of Waterville, Maine, a city of 15,000 or so in the center of the state. "The hospice volunteer is the one constant in the home during the end-of-life process," says executive director Dale Marie Clark, "because one volunteer is assigned and visits regularly, whereas the nurses and personal care attendants can vary from day to day."

Most care providers recognize and understand the importance of assigning a consistent team of caregivers to their clients. If you have concern, speak to the provider about this.

Volunteers, who have ranged in age from eighteen to eighty, are drawn to this service for a variety of reasons, says Clark. Some have experienced the death of a relative and want to help other survivors with what they have learned. Recently, college students who are entering the counseling or health care fields have joined the organization because they want training in the support of those who are dying and their families.

Because they are generally not medically licensed, volunteer responsibilities include such functions as help with transportation, household chores, and errands. The Waterville group also has among its volunteers fifteen massage therapists and others who practice relaxing and soothing body therapy.

The volunteers' most important function, however, is to listen and offer solace. "Many clients tend to protect family and friends, not wanting to burden them with their true feelings," observes Clark. "They find it easier to talk to strangers, so the volunteer becomes a sounding board." At the end of life, the volunteer can also become an important sounding board to the grieving family.

sources that guide you to hospice care at home will help you find such a residence.

Keep in mind, however, that although Medicare and Medicaid will continue to pay for hospice services in such a residence, they will not pay for routine room and board.[17] So she'll want to have some other means in place to help cover these and other such daily costs, since her out-of-pocket expenses could add up quickly.

You Need Comforting, Too. Hospice counselors will help comfort your mother and answer her questions about her condition. Make certain they counsel and comfort you as well. Among other things, they should prepare you for what is likely to happen at the time of death. Hollywood and the rest of the entertainment industry have schooled us to expect two kinds of death, either sudden and violent or a serene passage in which a bedridden patient slips quietly from smiling acceptance of her fate into eternal rest.

Most often, death happens neither way. Your loved one will perhaps slip into a nonresponsive state in the hours or days preceding death. It is very important for the hospice team to provide you with guidance at this time. If they fail to do so, don't hesitate to ask for it.

Help at the End. This is not pleasant to talk about and much less pleasant for the family to have to cope with alone. At the end of life, the sphincter muscle may relax, causing the body to release its fluids. Make sure to call the hospice agency immediately when death comes and that it responds quickly to come and clean your loved one's body. Even if you were in the calmest of emotional states—and you almost certainly will not be—it would still be difficult for you as an untrained layperson to deal with the end-of-life's grim, required routines.

When You Can't Be There

The dilemma is a familiar one. A friend's mother is dying. You don't want to pester her with a succession of phone calls when she has so much else on her mind. On the other hand, you fear that she might interpret your failure to call as a sign of indifference, when the truth is that you really do care about both her and her mother and want to offer moral support and maybe more.

So when Sona Mehring's close friend had a life-threatening pregnancy in 1997, Mehring came up with an inspiring solution to the dilemma, a website to keep family and friends informed about the critical situation, one that the pregnant friend in distress could update as she found the time. Mehring's resourceful stratagem has grown into CaringBridge, caringbridge.org, an Internet service that has enabled 150,000 families—and their number is growing—to create personalized websites through which family members and friends can exchange information with and provide support for those in crisis.

"The site also allows patients to be surrounded by a virtual group of family and friends at their bedside," observes Mehring, founder and executive director. "What a gift to those family and friends who can't be in the room." Some sites have continued as long as CaringBridge has been in existence," says Mehring, "to help families handle the grief and then enable them to remember the journey."

About a quarter of the sites are for seniors, says Mehring, an impressive showing for a generation more likely to be technophobic than younger generations. Notes Mehring: "I've heard some great stories about seniors who say, 'Wow, finally a good use for the computer.'"

You will need professionals at your side to help make funeral arrangements, obtain a death certificate, dispose of painkillers and other dangerous drugs, and take care of other details. And probably more urgent than any of the physical details of your mother's passing, you and other members of your family need help to deal with your grief.

Your mother's decline over a long period of time has likely exhausted and depressed you. But while she was alive, the necessity of using your body and mind to sustain hers kept you going. Now you have only grief and emptiness. In Chapter 14 we will talk about bereavement and how you and your family can go through it and emerge closer and stronger.

Hospice Care

Hospice is a special concept of care designed to provide comfort and support to patients and their families. Patients are referred to hospice when life expectancy is approximately six months or less. Hospice care can continue longer than six months if needed but requires physician certification.

Advantages
- Care is available twenty-four hours a day
- Care is provided by a team of professionals and volunteers
- Patient can avoid unwanted hospitalization and procedures

Disadvantages
- Aggressive treatments (aimed at treating an illness) are not part of regimen
- Can be emotionally wrenching process for patient and family to reach decision to pursue end-of-life care

- Family caregivers can be overwhelmed by responsibilities of providing hospice care

Choose This Option If
- Patient is diagnosed with a terminal illness and/or a projected life expectancy of six months or less
- Curative treatment is no longer an option
- Patient's primary needs become comfort care and symptom management

Average Annual Cost
- Hospice services are paid for through the Medicare hospice benefit, Medicaid hospice benefit, and most private insurers.
- If a person does not have coverage through Medicare, Medicaid, or a private insurance company, hospice will work with the person and their family to ensure needed services can be provided.

Resources Available
- Aging with Dignity, agingwithdignity.org
- American Hospice Foundation, americanhospice.org
- Americans for Better Care of the Dying, abcd-caring.org
- Dying Well, dyingwell.org
- Hospice Foundation of America, hospicefoundation.org
- Hospice Patients Alliance, hospicepatients.org
- International Association for Hospice & Palliative Care, hospicecare.com
- Medicare website (search for hospice), medicare.gov
- National Hospice and Palliative Care Organization, nhpco.org
- State hospice organizations

13

Funeral Services

This final gesture on behalf of the loved one is the act we all dread the most, the ending, the goodbye. And it would be foolish of us to pretend that the funeral is not a ceremony laden with grief and sadness. But there is another dimension to the funeral as well. It is a way of providing social support for you, the caregiver, and other family and friends, a first step in the bereavement process. It is a way to bring you and other family members, who have been enveloped in the care of your loved one for so long, back into the community and help make the transition to a new life.

Final Gesture

The funeral is also an opportunity for you and others to pay a final tribute to a loved one in a way that celebrates his or her uniqueness. As multiple alternatives for elder care have proliferated in recent decades, so have the options for a final parting. A funeral home in Odessa, Missouri, for example, offers a horse-drawn carriage as an alternative to a hearse.

When a Chicago dance instructor in his eighties died suddenly of a heart attack, his family first honored him with a small private funeral. A couple of months later the family held a memorial dance in his honor. About 350 friends and former students danced the night away, pausing from time to time as one of the dancers went to the microphone to recall moments of the departed's life.

Probably you won't come up with a tribute as grand and elaborate as a dance, but it is important for you to know that customs and laws have changed to give you considerable latitude in arranging a final farewell.

Religious Services

Services at places of worship, including churches and synagogues, have generally become somewhat more flexible, accommodating the wishes of the departed and their families. Talk with the clergy at the church at which you would like services for your loved one. Will you be able to choose the music and the Bible readings? How else will you and other family members and friends be able to participate?

Personalized Memorial Services. At many Christian churches, members of the family and friends are allowed to deliver the Bible readings as well as spoken and written tributes to the deceased. At a memorial service we attended in a Jewish synagogue not long ago, the proceedings were mostly a series of eulogies by friends who had known the deceased well at various stages of her life, from childhood through college and the workplace to motherhood and community service.

Funeral services don't have to be held in the morning or afternoon. In a nod to the reality that women as well as men have to report to an office during the day, services are frequently held at night. And it's helpful to remember that embalming is not mandatory if the body will be buried or cremated shortly after death—though funeral homes may require it for viewings or visitations.[1]

"Usually we have visitation and viewing the day before at the mortuary followed by the funeral at the church," says Bill, who has been a funeral director in the Omaha, Nebraska, area for four decades. "Normally most churches have some sort of structured service." But Bill goes on to note that he has dealt with some unusual requests over the years. "We've had motorcycles at funerals," he recalls. "We've played football fight songs, and we've taken people to the cemetery in the back of a fire truck, a pickup truck, and a hay rack."

Cremation Allowed. Most religious faiths now permit cremation, including the Roman Catholic Church, which for most of its history forbade it. You don't have to have an expensive cere-

> ## "Before I Go, You Should Know"
>
> Those who want to be sure that their wishes for an appropriate funeral are carried out should put those wishes in writing, advises the Funeral Consumers Alliance. The organization offers for $10 (in some areas free through local chapters) a funeral planning kit entitled "Before I Go, You Should Know" that recipients can distribute among family and friends. The kit includes a sixteen-page fill-in-the-blanks booklet for funeral plans, the location of important documents, computer passwords, and more. The kit also includes state-specific advance medical directives, giving instructions on what sort of intervention the recipient wants—and wants withheld—at the end of life.

mony or even use a funeral home. You can have a ceremony for your loved one at her home or your own, a revival of a practice that was the norm a century or so ago.[2]

The first step in planning a funeral is, of course, determining what your loved one would have wanted, another strong argument for urging him or her to create a will or at least put wishes in writing. The entire family should be brought into the planning, advises the Funeral Consumers Alliance, funerals.org, because, in the organization's experience, survivors have "found great meaning and peace carrying out thoughtful funeral plans that honored their family member in an appropriate and affordable way."[3]

Home Funeral

The home funeral is an alternative that can be attractive for several reasons, and a website, HomeFuneralDirectory.com, will help you arrange one. (Before you consider this option, however, make sure the front door is wide enough to admit the casket, a major obstruction, says funeral director Bill.) Family members, especially children, may experience less fear of death if the ceremony takes place at home, where they are free to mourn in their own way. Also, being physically involved in planning the service may help ease the grief. For many family members, it's a relief to be able to contribute their efforts rather than sit by idly as a professional funeral home staff takes charge. Also, a home funeral is economical. A dignified and loving home funeral can easily be held for less than $1,000.[4]

A drawback of the home funeral is that it may leave you and other family members with more details to handle than you would like. Someone has to arrange for such provisions as a death certificate, a casket, a burial site, and transportation. If you have used the services of a hospice agency, as described in the previous chapter, the agency will likely be able to help with such arrangements, as will the home funeral website homefuneral.info.

The Reasons for a Funeral?

Funerals, or at least death rituals, probably date back to the origins of man. We perform these because they help in ways such as the following:

- They help us to deal with our loss at a time of grief.
- They help us "release" the person who has died.
- They allow us to reflect on the past, deal with the present, and look to the future.
- They help to bind us together with other mourners, allowing for a possibility to share common thoughts, memories, and feelings.[5]

Picking the Funeral Home

However, most of the 2 million funerals conducted in the United States every year are done so under the auspices of a professional funeral director and home.[6] So, if that's the course you decide on, how do you pick the right home?

When making your decision, remember that many funeral providers offer various "packages" of goods and services that make up different kinds of funerals. When you arrange for a funeral, however, you have the right to buy goods and services separately. In other words, you do not have to accept a package that may include items you do not want; for instance, you may choose to buy a casket on your own rather than from the funeral home.[7]

Another consideration: you don't have to use the same funeral home the family has always used. For instance, you can check the NFDA directory (nfda.org) for a listing of local funeral homes and interview several before making your choice.[8]

Think Ahead

After the death, how long you can stay with the body may depend on where the death occurs. If it occurs at home, there is no need to move the body right away. If you have a list of people to notify, this is the time to call those who might want to come and see the body.[9]

As soon as possible, however, the death must be pronounced official by someone in authority like a doctor in a hospital or a hospice nurse. This person also fills out the necessary forms that will make it possible for the official death certificate to be prepared. If death happens at home without hospice, talk with the doctor, coroner, your local health department, or the funeral home representative in advance about how to proceed.[10]

Arrangements should be made to pick up the body as soon as the family is ready (usually this is done by the funeral home). If the death occurs in a hospital or nursing facility, they may call the funeral home for you. If it occurs at home, you will need to con-

Ten Important Facts About Funerals

- Funeral services don't have to be held in the morning or afternoon.
- In fact, evening services may better accommodate family and friends.
- The service can be held in your home (rather than a funeral home), where grief can be expressed more freely and personally.
- Embalming is not mandatory.
- A dignified funeral can be held for less than $2,000 (or even $1,000), although the average is between $6,000 and $10,000.
- A top-of-the-line casket can cost $10,000 or more.
- Cremation costs from $725 to $2,255.
- You don't have to use the entire package a funeral home may offer. Select only those services you need.
- You can (and should) ask the funeral director to break down the costs and eliminate anything you don't want or need.
- Many cemeteries require a concrete vault or grave liner—though these are not mandated by state law. This need not be a major additional expense. They can be purchased for as little as $200 with the average being about $400.

tact the funeral home directly—or ask a friend or family member to do that for you.[11]

Spiritual Tribute

Simultaneously, you have to anticipate and plan your spiritual tribute to your loved one. Ask yourself these questions, and to make sure you think about them clearly, write down the answers:

Get Help with the Details

Preoccupied with bigger concerns, caregivers often overlook some details until the last minute. Have another family member or friend help you with these:

- Contact relatives and friends immediately to give them time to prepare for the funeral services.
- Gather information for an obituary, including full name and nicknames, date of birth, occupation, military service, organizations, and names of survivors.
- Collect the names of organizations your loved one would like to receive donations in lieu of flowers.
- Select the clothing in which your loved one will be buried.
- Make arrangements for food or a reception after the burial service.
- Obtain a book for signatures for those who attend the funeral or memorial service. Also, provide a basket to collect calling cards.
- Select those who might deliver eulogies at the funeral or be pallbearers.
- Ask a neighbor or a security company to stay in the home while others attend the service—many robberies occur because a thief has been alerted to an opportunity by an obituary.

How can I create a service that celebrates Dad's life and accomplishments? How can I create one that will help me and the rest of the family express our grief and comfort one another? How can I ensure that Dad's body is treated with respect and is disposed of as he would have wished?

A traditional funeral usually costs about $6,000—including casket and vault. However, a more elaborate service can exceed $10,000 (this higher price typically would include "extras" such as obituary notices and limousines, and, in fact, some high-end caskets themselves can sell for $10,000 or more).[12]

Ask for Breakdowns

Don't hesitate to ask the funeral director to break down the costs. A funeral service is both an act of devotion and a business transaction. If you don't feel up to negotiating with the funeral director, ask your brother-in-law or someone else not related by blood to your loved one to do so. Also, be aware that funeral directors will likely require some payments up front. The costs typically come in three parts:

- A basic service fee, which clients cannot decline, for planning the funeral, the services of the funeral director and attendants, coordinating with the cemetery for burial, and various permits.
- Optional services, which clients can decline, such as transporting the body, embalming, use of the home for viewing, ceremony, or service, and the use of a limousine or hearse.
- Cash advances for services provided by those outside the funeral home, which clients can also decline, such as flowers, obituary notices, clergy, pallbearers, and musicians.[13]

Bear in mind that while you may consider it an unnecessary expense to pay the funeral home to guarantee the services in the third category, it may be well worth the cost if you'd like to ensure that your loved one's obituary is written and placed in

Painful, but Plan Ahead

In many ways death was the easy part, Jim recalls of the passing of his wife, Diana. She died of cancer relatively quickly, and the hospice agency was helpful in arranging for her body to be picked up by the mortuary. The most difficult part followed. Jim and his family had not planned ahead, so all the decisions had to be made quickly and, generally, in a state of powerful emotions. How expensive should the casket be? Very expensive, Jim considered, as his wife of thirty-two years and mother of his three children deserved. Inexpensive, he reconsidered, because Diana was a lady of modest tastes. He chose a casket in the mid-price range, as he assumes most families do.

The decisions were endless—order of service, obituary notice, final clothing, floral arrangements, and on and on. Then there was the inevitable issue of payment. Would Jim sign over Diana's insurance benefits to the mortuary? No, Diana had no such insurance. In that case the mortuary demanded a deposit. Jim also misunderstood the amount required by the cemetery, which would not allow the burial to proceed without payment in full. Fortunately, Jim's son-in-law had his checkbook and covered the balance.

Jim was left feeling he had been exploited by mercenaries. But the real lesson of his experience is that the family caregiver should plan ahead. As it became clear that his wife's death was only weeks away, Jim, understandably stunned by grief, should have had a friend or a less emotionally distraught family member, that son-in-law perhaps, call prospective mortuaries and the cemetery and inquire about schedules and payments.

local newspapers and that the musicians are paid, details that you may not want to deal with in the midst of your grief.

The Burial Site

After services at either home or a place of worship, the funeral party generally proceeds to the burial site. The cost of burial will be based upon a number of variables such as location; for instance, plots can be especially expensive in metropolitan areas. This charge also will cover the cost of digging the grave and filling it in after the ceremony (keep in mind that U.S. veterans are entitled to a free burial in a national cemetery, with a grave marker—as are some civilian military personnel and selected Public Health Service employees).[14]

Many cemeteries also require a concrete vault or grave liner to prevent the ground from settling, though these are not actually mandated by state law. When pricing these items, compare several before selecting a model—also a good idea when purchasing a monument or marker.[15]

The Cremation Alternative

At a time when we are increasingly concerned about the environment, cremation seems more ecologically sound. Cremation is also substantially less expensive, especially in urban areas where the shortage of available land drives up the cost of burial sites; the cost of a plot or crypt is included only if the remains are buried or entombed.[16]

Prices for cremation, not including the price of an urn, range from $725 to $2,255.[17] Urns can be interred in a family cemetery plot or kept at a family member's home or in another appropriate memorial setting. Sometimes family members scatter the ashes over a place the loved one considered especially important, a place where he or she felt most complete. That can be a deeply moving gesture, but be aware of local government restrictions before you do so.

Look Back with Satisfaction

The funeral is over. The loved one has been buried or cremated. Now the difficult part begins, say many survivors. The hours and days and months, perhaps even years, have been filled with the rewards of taking care of your failing loved one. The burden has been heavy but satisfying. You have given your mother, or father, your most loving, most energetic, most resourceful best, through periods that were confusing and harrowing. Now it is all over. Your siblings, cousins, and friends go back to their own homes, as do you. It is quiet. Empty.

In the next chapter, we will talk about how to deal with the bereavement that accompanies the emptiness.

14

Bereavement

Bereavement is possibly the most trying period you will have to go through in the process of caring. Before your loved one's death, you might have told yourself how relieved you would be when the ordeal of dying and the funeral were over. But now the funeral is over, and you may not be relieved. You are bereft, adrift, depressed, and anxious.

The Reality of Grief

As your loved one declined week by week, day by day, you were saddened, but you had a role, a function. Now there are no doctors to call, no professional caregivers to interview, no nursing homes to inspect. There is no assignment, no crisis to distract you. There is emptiness. One of the greatest losses a caregiver can face is the loss of purpose. For many, caregiving has been a long and excruciating task and yet a fulfilling one that gave additional meaning to life.

In theory, the death of an elderly parent should be relatively easy for you to accept, a loss much less calamitous than that of a child or a spouse. It is, after all, the natural order of things. Parents are supposed to die before their children. Consider the extraordinary pain your parents would have suffered if they had to watch you decline and die. It is hard to imagine a greater grief. So the knowledge that you will survive, raise their grandchildren, continue to honor them, and cherish memories of them has spared them the terrifying anguish of outliving you.

And most children do come to terms with the death of their parents. But it is hardly as easy as it seems theoretically for many reasons, including the feeling of helplessness at the loss of the person who may have been at your side all your life, much longer than your spouse or children. "I don't know how I will go on," one woman said in contemplating the imminent death of her ninety-five-year-old father. "I talk with him every day."

Don't Be Surprised by Guilt

Some survivors have to struggle with very different emotions, such as guilt over not making peace with a parent who was distant or even cruel, or even guilt because they feel relief that the alienated parent is gone. Or, a son might be angry with himself for not insisting that the doctors pay more attention to his mother's needs or angry with his dead father for not taking better care of himself.

"It is extremely common for the person who is grieving to be critical of himself or herself for either doing something to or not doing something for the person who has died or left," observe the writers of the helpful website athealth.com. "It is not unusual for the grieving person to be angry toward others, especially other family members or God."[1]

Intensity of Feelings

During the grief process, many people are surprised to experience the strongest feelings they have felt in their lives—numbness, sadness, loneliness, guilt, shock, anxiety, depression, and agitation among them.

Those emotions can be directed toward numerous people. "In the death of a parent, what we see most often is tension among siblings," says Joy Johnson, cofounder of the Centering Corporation, a nonprofit organization dedicated to providing education and resources for the bereaved. "I believe there is no such thing as a fully functional family, so there are going to be some angry spots. The primary caregiver says, 'My sister who has never come in from out of town to see Mom has now come and is taking over the funeral planning as well as mom's best possessions and has no thanks for me, the sibling who is worn to a frazzle.'"

The sibling from out of town may be dealing with a different kind of anger, such as a belief that no one in the family appreci-

---

Dealing with Grief: Letting Others Help

In time it will pass, but before that happens, there are some measures you can take that will help ease the pain:

- Contact other family members and close friends. Gather a circle of people who will provide emotional support.
- Notify your spiritual leader, such as a pastor, priest, or rabbi. Let them know if you want the funeral or memorial service at your place of worship.
- Call the funeral home you have chosen. Let them know of any special services you may need. If you have not already done so, notify the hospital about which funeral home will be serving you.
- Have a relative, friend, or neighbor answer the phone or help with phone calls if there are many people to notify.
- Have someone keep a list of all phone calls received, flowers, and food donations.[2]

---

ates how difficult and expensive it is to travel 3,000 miles, or her long-simmering fury because her suggestions for Mom's care were always ignored. And she is grieving too.

Wide Mood Swings

People grieve in highly individualized ways. For some people, interspersed among the low and painful periods are brief bursts of almost ecstatic and enthusiastic feelings, the Athealth website notes, that can lead to feelings of guilt. So take comfort in the knowledge that you are not alone. Wide mood swings are a normal part of bereavement. If you regret that you were not closer to your mother at the end of her life, write a letter to her as if she were alive explaining your feelings, and then write what you think she would say in a reply to you.[3]

Grieving Physically

"Everyone's grief is different and depends on the relationship," Johnson continues. "If the adult child has been abused, unloved, or worn to a frazzle, the grief is diminished and there's more relief. Death after a long-term illness brings a combination of grief and relief." We grieve physically too. "My experience shows that we are more likely to get a cold after the death of anyone close to us." There is, in truth, a "broken heart" syndrome, which is not a heart attack, but nonetheless a condition of bereavement that causes chest pain.

Now let's talk about your grief and the bereavement processes that will help you cope with it. We will give you this warning at the start. If the grief becomes crippling to the point that you can't carry out normal daily activities, perhaps you spend all day in bed, that is cause for alarm. Sometimes the grieving person may need medications for depression if the depression becomes severe or if it lasts for more than a couple of months. Also, medications are helpful to the person suffering from prolonged insomnia or excessive anxiety associated with grief.[4]

Don't Go It Alone

Most children who lose parents don't require long-term medication, although they might need the help of prescription sleeping pills for a brief period. Nor do most survivors need profound and prolonged counseling. "Keep a journal and write down your feelings," advises Johnson of the Centering Corporation. "Talk to your journal. It's a cheap psychiatrist. Every day write down one thing that brings you comfort and one thing that brings you joy."

Leo's Journal

Diane and Leo had been married for sixteen years when terminal cancer struck Diane. During her fight for life, Leo created a website through CaringBridge, an Internet service that has enabled families to create personalized websites through which relatives and friends can exchange information and support for those in crisis. (For more about CaringBridge, see Chapter 12.) He kept friends up to date on her condition. When Diane passed away, Leo briefly thought about shutting down the website. But then he wisely concluded that by keeping it open and active he could chronicle, process, and ultimately dissipate his grief by creating a journal to share with friends. Here are excerpts from Leo's Web journal:

Wednesday, July 9
This will be my last posting on this site, so it might be lengthy as there are a lot of things that I want to say but will be unable to express them to you at the visitation and funeral. Diane fought a good fight. She didn't want to leave me and all of you. Over the last week, we talked, and she said she wasn't afraid for herself but was rather afraid for me.

Tuesday, July 22
I have changed my mind about continuing the journal. Several people have told me how much this has helped them in their grief over Diane's going to Heaven.

I had a breakthrough in thought last week while talking to our old friend Pam. We had prayed for total healing for Diane. I had thought that God had not answered our prayers, but He did. She wanted to go home, and He took her to be with Him.

Tuesday, July 29
I put a photo of Diane on the photo page and will add more as I get some time. I should have done it a long time ago.

Wednesday, August 6
Everything seems to be going okay. My daily routines are changing for the better, and if I could just fix my sleep pattern, that would be great. . . . The biggest change in my life right now is in trusting my own judgment on changes to make in my life.

Tuesday, October 7
Today is three months of life without Diane being physically here. She is here with me 24/7 in my heart and my memories. I hope that all of you, her friends and family, are doing okay. She would have wanted your sadness and grief to diminish over time and for you to get on with living a good and happy life.

Journaling has a cathartic effect, an opportunity to express privately your deepest inner emotions in a way least subject to the review or judgment of others but still providing a necessary outlet for your emotions.

You do need the help of others. Don't try to "tough it out" in the false belief that it is a sign of great strength to go it alone. Find a talking buddy. Don't be embarrassed to cry in the company of friends and family, or strangers for that matter. "Reach out for physical help and ask to be taken to lunch," says Johnson. "Seek out emotional help by asking people to call you once a day to check in. We had a friend who asked people to trace around their hands and write on the drawing of the hand what they would be willing to do for her, and then she collected on it. Do what fulfills you and gives you joy and comfort. We need our own kind of distraction and our own kind of quiet."

Seek out the comfort of your religious community. Find other local grief support groups, which you can locate through churches, health clinics, the YMCA, or similar organizations. Again, do not go through bereavement alone.

While each person's journey of grieving is unique, there are some common emotional expressions of grief. These include sadness, loneliness, anger, guilt and blame, anxiety, and finally relief. The key is finding safe and acceptable ways to express grief so that you can move through the process, in your own way.[5]

Grief: Normal or Excessive

Grief is an inevitable consequence of loss. Some manifestations are normal and will pass. Other symptoms are more serious and may require psychiatric or other treatment. It is normal to

- be sad and depressed
- have insomnia
- eat too much or too little
- experience crying spells
- experience mood swings
- have difficulty concentrating
- withdraw from social life for a time

It is *not* normal to

- feel worthless
- feel severe guilt
- forget appointments repeatedly
- lose ability to function
- contemplate suicide[6]

Memories Soften

Attempts to ignore grief and avoid reminders of a deceased parent are not healthy, even though avoidance might minimize distress early on; it generally invites greater psychological problems later. The realities of day-to-day living are that you are going to pass in the street someone who looks like your father or be reminded of your mother's favorite food when you walk down an aisle in the supermarket. "We call those situations TUGs, which stands for Totally Unexpected Grief," says Johnson. "Christmas brings a lot of TUGs."

But over time those painful encounters are transformed into positive experiences. "Memories evolve from sad to bittersweet to pleasant," says Johnson. "When I hear a wren sing, I think of my mother. We've also discovered that adult children who had terrible relationships with their parents sometimes develop good ones when their parents are gone. The bad memories soften, and they remember better times."

Bereavement is an inevitable reaction to grievous loss. Ask others to help you get through it and ask them immediately. If you wait for six months before deciding you can't go through the grief alone, friends are more likely to be puzzled by why you are still struggling and perhaps be less sympathetic. And keep looking forward to that time when your grief will have subsided, to that time when you will smile to hear a wren sing.

15

Complicating Ailments and Issues

Until now, we have concentrated on progressive stages in the aging process and given your loved one and you, the caregiver, advice about how you should think about each stage and the appropriate settings. Our journey has taken us from aging in place, in which a senior remains fully independent and in robust health, through hospice care. We have ordered the chapters sequentially, as though you were dealing with your loved one's physical and mental health as it declined over time.

Here we're going to change the focus a bit and look at a cluster of ailments and loss of skills that can occur at any time through the stages of decline. These ailments compound and sometimes disguise life-threatening health problems and also complicate the care of your loved one. This cluster is sometimes known as the "geriatric syndromes," and seniors frequently suffer from more than one of the syndromes. In this chapter, we will define each component, explain how it can make care more difficult, and make suggestions about how to treat it.

Components of Geriatric Syndromes

Here we rely largely on an authority at the University of Nebraska Medical Center, Jane F. Potter, M.D., the Harris Professor of Geriatric Medicine at the medical center's department of internal medicine and recent past president of the American Geriatrics Society. The good news about the geriatric syndromes, says Potter, is that there are interventions and treatments that can lessen their effects. "These conditions limit the quality of life," she notes. And, if not attended to properly, they also limit independence—something of great importance to seniors. Unfortunately, you cannot always count on your mother's physician to identify and treat them. That puts an additional burden on the family caregiver. The purpose of this chapter is to alert you to special situations that require your attention and advocacy with health care providers.

"When you go to a doctor, he pays attention to your high blood pressure, diabetes, whatever," Potter says, "but he doesn't always focus on these other conditions."

Side Effects of Multiple Medications

Many seniors take a variety of drugs to treat an array of problems, such as high blood pressure, high cholesterol, loss of bone mass, Parkinson's disease, or any number of other serious conditions. Such a combination of drugs is referred to as *polypharmacy*, and the result for the patient can be extreme confusion, or worse. "What I tell medical students is that every symptom or problem in their older patients may be due to a drug side effect. When an older person complains of dizziness, anxiety, depression, or

What You Need to Know About Your Medicine Cabinet

By Dima M. Qato, University of Chicago pharmacist and lead researcher on a study of pharmaceutical dangers for seniors, and Stacy Tessler Lindau, M.D., senior author of study.

- **What is the biggest danger that seniors face from their medications and supplements?** The biggest dangers that seniors face from their medications and supplements are not knowing why they're taking them and not knowing whether they are safe to take in combination. Seniors, like all people, need to be active participants in their health care, and they need to ask their physicians and pharmacists why they are taking a certain drug, what the side effects are, and whether it's safe with the other prescription and nonprescription products they are using.

(continued)

- **What are some common misconceptions about medications?** Some may assume that just because a drug is available without a prescription (e.g., a dietary supplement or over-the-counter drug), it's safe. Likewise, patients may erroneously assume that their physician or pharmacist is aware of all the medications they take. Therefore, patients need to know that while medications are often beneficial, there can be risks associated with their use, particularly in combination with other drugs. If they need to self-medicate with an over-the-counter drug or dietary supplement, they should consult with a physician or pharmacist first and specifically ask whether it's OK to use a new product given the medications they're already taking.

- **Are there any resources that are a good starting point for someone concerned about the senior medication question?** Yes. The National Institutes of Health's online database of drugs and supplements is an important reference for anyone concerned about the safety of their medication regimen: nlm.nih.gov/medlineplus/druginformation.html. However, patients should be encouraged to discuss all concerns with their physician before starting or stopping a medication, as the risks and benefits associated with specific drugs and drug combinations vary depending on a patient's clinical profile.

- **What is the best way for seniors to prevent the confusion that can arise from multiple prescriptions and treatment strategies that result from different medical conditions and the need for many different physicians in the mix?** Physicians and pharmacists need to ask their patients about all the medications they use—prescription and nonprescription—and patients need to be prepared to share this information with their physician. Carrying a list of all medications in a wallet or purse can be helpful. Getting their prescriptions filled at one pharmacy or pharmacy chain can help maintain a centralized comprehensive profile of the medications prescribed by their multiple physicians and specialists.

Medicine Safety Starting Points

- If you need to self-medicate with over-the-counter drugs or supplements, consult with your doctor or pharmacist *first*.
- Take the initiative and ask your doctor about medication interactions any time you start using a new drug.
- Ideally fill your prescriptions at one pharmacy or pharmacy chain (so that access to your prescription information is centralized and can be adequately assessed).
- Tell your doctor and pharmacist about *all* the medications you use—prescription and nonprescription.
- Just because a drug can be acquired without a prescription *does not mean* that drug is safe for you.
- A daily or weekly pillbox carefully prepared and reviewed by a pharmacist, nurse, or geriatrician can make it easier and safer for seniors to take multiple medications and supplements.

Source: Dima M. Qato; G. Caleb Alexander; Rena M. Conti; et al. "Use of Prescription and Over-the-Counter Medications and Dietary Supplements Among Older Adults in the United States," *JAMA* 300, no. 24 (2008): 2867–78.

bladder problems, look at their meds as a possible cause of the problem," says Potter.

Sometimes the first clue that polypharmacy is a problem is that the senior becomes puzzled about when she is supposed to be taking the medications and how: If they have to be taken every four hours, should I set the alarm clock to wake me in the middle of the night? Are these the pills that are supposed to be taken on an empty stomach or after eating? The label says to take one three times per day, but I'm sure the doctor said to take three once a day.

The solution in part may be to get a pill organizer, Potter suggests. Sometimes prescriptions have accrued over time, and both the senior and the family caregiver have forgotten why she is taking some of them. Go to the physician and the pharmacist and say, "The medication schedule is too complicated. What can we do to simplify the number of drugs and the dosing schedule?"

Anxiety and Depression

Among U.S. adults aged sixty-five and older, depression and anxiety are two of the most common mental health problems.[1] Depression, which actually tops this list, can interfere with seniors' physical, mental, and social functioning—and it can have a negative effect on the course and treatment of other diseases, along with causing unnecessary doctor and emergency-room visits. However, while the rate of older adults with depressive symptoms tends to increase with age—for instance, leading to unusually high suicide rates among older men—depression should *not* be considered a normal part of growing older. Rather, about four of every five of these cases are treatable.[2]

The symptoms of depression can be sadness and loss of interest in life and previously enjoyable activities. Perhaps your loved one was usually upbeat and took adversity in stride but is now anxious, blue, and low—all possible indications of a serious disorder. But both depression and anxiety can take a different form, such as personality change or an exaggeration of a previous trait. "Maybe Mom was merely a nervous Nellie before," says Potter, "but now small things create severe stress."

Depression and anxiety clearly upset the routine of care for a senior. He becomes unwilling to see the doctor or take his medications, eat properly, or go to the senior center. Tell his primary

John Battles Night Fright

John, who lived by himself in Las Cruces, New Mexico, remained remarkably active at the age of 100. His problem came at night, when anxiety and nervousness disturbed his sleep, a part of the senior syndrome sometimes known as "night fright." Thoughts and memories kept him awake. "There's lots of things that go across my mind about what I used to be able to do that I can't anymore," John said. He was no longer able to do the carpentry he so enjoyed.

Many share John's problem. Studies have shown that many adults over the age of fifty do not get a good night's sleep every night of the week. Physiological problems accompanying age, such as a decreased amount of time spent in some stages of sleep, seem to explain the anxiety in part. Also, seniors who are frail worry more about getting help during the night than during the day. In one study, patients with dementia suffering with night fright were helped by being exposed to bright light for a period during either the morning or evening. John was helped by the company of a professional caregiver around the clock, who talked or sometimes played dominoes with him. "I don't usually win," reported one of the caregivers.

doctor about this changed behavior and that you think he might be suffering from depression. Both medication and counseling are effective treatments for depression. Also, encourage your loved one to keep up friendships and get together with her peers as often as she can. Activities, exercise, and socialization help to speed recovery from depression.

Dementia

After age eighty-five, nearly half of seniors will have some cognitive impairment or dementia, typically Alzheimer's. This brain disorder makes it difficult for people to remember, learn, and communicate and over time makes it increasingly difficult for seniors to take care of themselves.[3] Victims of dementia suffer symptoms such as memory loss, a decline in the ability to perform routine tasks or learn new ones, and a loss of language, judgment, and planning skills. Alzheimer's can even bring about personality changes[4]—for instance, in the case of a formerly sociable senior who might stop going to parties, church, and other events.

What to Look For. Mildred had been a gregarious hostess who happily fawned over her many guests from the beginning of the party to the end. So her family was shocked when she let it be known that the plans for her eightieth birthday party frightened her. The big party was cancelled, and a much smaller one substituted. It wasn't until some weeks later that it became apparent that Mildred's short-term memory had deteriorated markedly.

Dementia can interfere with the care of a loved one in a number of ways. People with dementia may eat poorly and irregularly and ignore exercise and social activity, all functions that would likely improve their health. Family caregivers are the first to recognize that dementia may be developing and should seek medical evaluation as soon as symptoms are recognized.

Alzheimer's Disease. Alzheimer's disease is the most common—and a heartbreaking—form of dementia, afflicting only about 5 percent of seniors between sixty-five and seventy-four. But nearly half of those over the age of eighty-five may be affected.[5] The disease usually begins slowly with mild memory loss and develops gradually into crippling brain damage with symptoms that can include paranoia. Ellen, a widow in her eighties, was convinced that professional caregivers in the house were plotting against her and stealing her jewelry.

Alzheimer's victims typically live for eight to ten years after being diagnosed with the disease and sometimes for as long as twenty years.[6] So far, no medication or treatment has been successful in reversing or stopping Alzheimer's, although medications are available that may help delay progression of some of the symptoms.[7] It remains perhaps the most difficult condition to cope with in a family setting. Contact the Alzheimer's Association, at alz.org, for information on support groups in your area.

Falls and Lack of Mobility

Did your mother used to keep up with you when you walked briskly through the supermarket but now trails well behind you with an uncertain gait? That laggardness is not simply a natural slowing with age. It could be brought on by Parkinson's disease, poor nutrition, arthritis, or even an undetected minor stroke. And it is not normal. It is dangerous and often a precursor to falls. Among older adults, falls are the leading cause of traumatic brain injuries and deaths by injury. The risk of being gravely injured increases with age, and people over seventy-five who fall are four to five times more likely than others to be admitted to a long-term care facility for longer than a year with a broken hip or other major injury.[8]

Lifestyle as a Preventative. So if your loved one shows signs of a halting or shuffling step, treat the condition seriously and inform his physician. Seek referral to a physical therapist. Good diet and regular exercise are preventatives. Traditional exercise regimens emphasize aerobics, strength, and flexibility. That's fine for all ages, but a workout routine for seniors should include a program to improve balance as well.

Parkinson's Disease. One percent of the population over sixty suffers from a restriction on their mobility known as Parkinson's disease, a disorder of the central nervous system that causes tremors or trembling of limbs, rigid limbs, stooped posture, and a shuffling gait.[9] Households of those with Parkinson's disease should be rearranged to reduce the likelihood of falls, including getting rid of thick rugs, which are difficult to walk over for those with a shuffling gait. Lamps should be placed where they cannot be easily tipped over. Chairs and other pieces of furniture should be separated to create an easy passage for walkers and wheelchairs.[10]

Vision Loss

Declining eyesight and hearing, two of the most common handicaps of the senior years, are not only limiting in themselves, they can also complicate and aggravate other conditions. A loved one with a halting step is much more likely to trip if he cannot see an obstacle clearly. A loved who does not hear well might misunderstand a doctor's instructions or miss a shout or bell that signals danger.

Cataracts. One of the most common vision problems among seniors is cataracts, a clouding that develops in the crystalline lens of the eye resulting in varying degrees of opacity, from slight to complete. Over time seniors with cataracts can lose some of their driving skills, especially their ability to drive at night. On unfamiliar roads, they find it difficult to read signs at a distance or distinguish the stripes on the highway. Ask your parents in a non-alarmist way if they have noticed that it is becoming more difficult to drive at night. The decline can be so gradual that they might not pay serious attention until you ask them to think about it.

A Better Lightbulb. Fortunately, cataracts can almost always be fixed by simple surgery. Some vision problems, including difficulty reading, are even easier to remedy. Many of today's seniors grew up in the Great Depression when people commonly tried to save money by using low-wattage lightbulbs, Potter notes. Such habits are hard to break. Make your parents a gift of bright, but energy-efficient, environmentally sound lightbulbs. They will read with much less strain.

Other vision problems, however, are not so simply corrected. Glaucoma and macular degeneration are two very serious eye impairments that strike the old disproportionately and can severely limit their sight. People over sixty-five should have their vision checked annually, Potter advises.

Hearing Loss

A decline of hearing can be even more subtle than diminishing vision, with consequences that can include depression, a feeling of isolation, and even a decline of memory and cognition. Conversation, listening to music, and tuning into news broadcasts stimulate the brain. One early sign of seriously impaired hearing, says Potter, is a loss of interest in group conversations.

Imagine a senior sitting at a table with family or friends in a noisy restaurant. The younger guests at the table can screen out the background noise, but not the senior. He finds himself in a sea of babble. Even his family and friends seem to be speaking an unintelligible language. He wants to go home.

Some seniors are embarrassed to talk to younger family members about hearing loss. Maybe that's because the cartoon figure holding a horn to his ear has long been a symbol of the decrepitude of age. When a doctor or nurse gives your father instructions about how to care for himself at home, he might simply pretend that he has heard and understood everything that was said.

Talk to your parents about their hearing loss, and learn to accommodate those difficulties. Make an effort to face them when you speak, speak more slowly, and raise your voice slightly but do not yell. Women, in particular, should be aware that a high-pitched female voice is especially hard to hear. Respect your parents' wishes not to dine at the restaurant with the blaring music; get a corner table and let your older relative have her back against the wall. One piece of good news is that the new generation of hearing aids is more effective than preceding ones, although still quite expensive.

Incontinence

The condition often starts as the need to urinate more frequently and eventually results in the loss of bladder control. Incontinence can cause those who suffer from it to withdraw from their social circle and isolate themselves from others, exacerbating problems of depression and anxiety. Potter is working with a woman who has dropped out of bridge club because of bladder troubles. Medications can help certain forms of incontinence, Potter says, but the first step in treatment is always a behavioral program, which consists of regular toileting on a schedule, learning to control urgency, adequate but not excessive fluid intake, and pelvic muscle (Kegel) exercises. Most communities have physical therapists who help guide older people in learning behavioral programs. Ask your older relative's physician for a referral.

Malnutrition

You can see that your mother is losing weight. Her clothing doesn't fit; nor do her dentures. Perhaps she has a serious illness, but even if she does not, it is important to address weight loss. Weight loss is not part of normal aging, and it can be a sign of frailty. Maybe she has increased difficulty shopping or cooking; maybe food is no longer appealing because she can no longer smell or taste it, a common problem among older people. Your mother may need help preparing food in a way that it will be appetizing again. Many in-home care businesses provide meal preparation services that can help address malnutrition issues and help assure that healthy and appetizing meals are available.

Obesity

The polar-opposite condition is obesity, which is considered by many experts to be a national epidemic. Seniors who live alone, who are tired of cooking, or whose taste and smell are impaired may rely on convenience foods that are high in sugar, salt, or fat.

Unfortunately, however, obesity is a risk factor for many chronic conditions, including four of the ten leading causes of death in the United States: coronary heart disease, type 2 diabetes, stroke, and several forms of cancer. Obesity also can worsen conditions such as arthritis, and it is associated with the limiting of activities and feelings of sadness and hopelessness.[11] It has even been implicated as a potential precursor to cognitive decline in seniors.[12]

Diabetes

Obesity is a major cause of type 2 diabetes, a devastating disease that has an impact on almost every part of the body and can lead to blindness, cardiovascular disease, stroke, kidney failure, amputations, and nerve damage. Some of the warnings that caregivers should be aware of are fatigue, frequent urination, increased thirst, blurred vision, and the slow healing of wounds.[13]

Diabetes is treated by the management of glucose levels through a combination of medication, insulin injections, and lifestyle changes. Caregivers of diabetes sufferers have to know which foods can quickly raise blood sugar, as well as how changes in diet and exercise routines can affect diabetes. Exercise, including walking, is also important for controlling diabetes.[14]

Persistent Pain

Up to half of seniors living at home have pain every day, which can be caused by arthritis, an old fracture, a stroke, diabetes, shingles, or other ailments. Not only is the pain tortuous in itself, but it can aggravate other conditions. A senior in pain is less likely to pursue the exercise program that has improved his general health; he is more likely to use painkillers, some of which cause side effects. As a rule, treatment is aimed at keeping pain under control. Waiting until pain is severe makes it more difficult to treat. For example, treatment with extended-release acetaminophen every eight hours often controls pain and avoids the need for a narcotic painkiller. People with persistent pain are at high risk of becoming depressed. Have a doctor check your father out. He might get relief by something as simple as a modification of his exercise program or a topical rub. But other sufferers may need a major intervention, such as hip or knee replacement.

Sleep Disorders

Getting older is frequently accompanied by a change in sleep patterns that can prevent a senior from getting proper rest. Perhaps your loved one complains of difficulty falling asleep or wakes up during the night or too early in the morning. He compensates by taking more than one normal hour-long nap during the day and, therefore, sleeps even less during the night. Poor sleep may be a symptom of depression or anxiety; or poor sleep may aggravate these conditions. The first step in treatment is good sleep hygiene, which includes eliminating just-before-bedtime routines that tend to make people more alert, such as exercise or a shower. A heavy meal right before bed also interferes with sleep. But people should not go to bed hungry, so a light snack may be helpful. Also, the senior should develop a good sleep routine, which includes going to bed and getting up at the same time every day.

Resources

Any of the conditions we have discussed in this chapter can rob a senior of a high quality of life. So be aware of them and don't hesitate to bring them to the attention of physicians and other professional caregivers. The resources in the following list will provide more information that will help you in your quest to be an advocate for your loved one's health.

- Alzheimer's Association, alz.org
- American Geriatrics Society Foundation for Health in Aging, "Aging in the Know," healthinaging.org/agingintheknow
- American Pain Society, ampainsoc.org
- American Parkinson's Disease Association, apdaparkinson.org
- American Physical Therapy Association's Section on Geriatrics, geriatricspt.org/clients/resources.cfm
- American Psychiatric Association, psych.org

- Better Hearing Institute, betterhearing.org
- Geriatric Mental Health Foundation, gmhfonline.org/gmhf
- Lighthouse International, lighthouse.org
- National Institute of Mental Health, nimh.nih.gov
- National Institute on Aging, nih.gov/nia
- National Institute on Aging, "AgePage: A Good Night's Sleep," niapublications.org/agepages/sleep.asp
- National Association for Continence, www.nafc.org

16

Difficult Situations

While writing this book, we have hoped that through all the challenges of caregiving, you will be working with cooperative relatives; that your parents are not only grateful for your help but demonstrate their gratitude and do what they can to make your labors on their behalf easier; and that your siblings appreciate your efforts as well and pitch in cheerfully to help.

But we know that the world is not always so tidy and supportive. Even though you and your parents love one another, you may be separated emotionally from one another by differing temperaments or ancient quarrels. The way you choose to live has disappointed them, perhaps. Or maybe you still resent their attempts to control your life. Your younger brother has always resisted your inclination to take charge, even though he has never shown any willingness to accept responsibility himself. And so on. Probably no family works smoothly all the time, and many families are troubled by strife of various kinds.

Antagonisms Can Get Worse

It would be wonderful indeed if the crisis of caregiving would dissolve old conflicts and bring everyone together in a noble cause. Unfortunately, the crisis is not likely to accomplish that, at least not immediately, and not without a lot of work. If anything, old antagonisms are likely to get worse in the urgency, and sometimes emergency, of caregiving.

If your father was stubborn as a middle-aged adult, he is more likely to become mulish rather than mellow as a senior. If your mother was wary of the unfamiliar before, as the years go on she may become downright suspicious of strangers, or even paranoid about them. Again, the earlier you can get your parents to face difficult decisions like those involved in drafting a will or structuring long-term care insurance, the better.

How do you prepare yourself for battles that may come? We offer advice in this chapter about how to deal with some specific situations that arise frequently, but first we suggest that you try to construct a philosophical framework for dealing with difficult family situations in general.

Recognize that not all of the friction between you and your parents is the result of clashing personalities or expectations or has anything to do with all of you as individuals. Old age is accompanied by at least some pain and if not by outright fatigue, some weariness. Daily chores seem more annoying than they used to be. Even the best-natured seniors get angry from time to time over trivial obstructions.

If your relationship with your mother has been strained for a long time, make it clear to her that you would like to start over. Find an expression you're comfortable with, such as "I know we've had problems getting along, but I'd like to do it differently from now on." Use the expression repeatedly if you have to, until the point gets through to her.

When you ask siblings and other relatives to help, try to match their talents and dispositions to the task. Don't ask your brother to bathe your mother just so that he can experience firsthand what you go through every day in dealing with incontinence. He'll resent you and her. Let him get his hands dirty by clearing the old paint cans and rusty power tools out of the basement.

Advice on Some Common Parent-Child Conflicts

Here we've listed some tough situations that have come up again and again in our experience working with caregivers and their families. We have asked for guidance from experts in two fields: Phyllis Mensh Brostoff, president of the board of the National Association of Professional Geriatric Care Managers, and Adriane Berg, CEO of Generation Bold—a consultant on reaching boomers and seniors—and author of *How Not to Go Broke at 102!*

"Work with Me"

A friend we'll call George has parents whose demands were difficult to satisfy. Some years ago, one of them suffered a serious illness that left him somewhat disabled. George's mother felt not only burdened by the disaster, which is understandable, but furious at having to deal with it alone. George, an only child, was a young man at the time, beginning a life and a career in another city far away.

George and his wife visited his parents when they could and did their best to assist them from afar. For instance, George and his wife helped to arrange care for George's parents, provided guidance, and were always available to talk on the phone. But no matter how much George and his wife gave, the relationship with his parents was strained.

Although he knew he was doing the right thing by staying with his new city and his job, George felt the tug of obedience and duty to his parents. So George put up with the situation. But on one visit during which they became particularly angry with him, he and his wife politely but unexpectedly walked out right in the middle of a contentious conversation.

It was their first dramatic protest, and it had a satisfying result. From that point on, George insisted in return that he be recognized by his parents as an adult, not a child to be ordered about. "Work with me" became his operative phrase when dealing with them. Relations are not yet perfect, but they are better. George only wishes that he had thought of "Work with me" many years ago.

Your Father Won't Surrender the Car Keys

This is one of the most frequent family dilemmas. Your father stubbornly insists that he can drive as well as he ever did, but the evidence tells you otherwise. There are dents in the side of his car you believe to be the result of fender benders he has not mentioned to you.

Your first step could be to accompany him while he drives so you see firsthand what could be the cause of his accidents. His problem could simply be a loss of hearing or a vision problem that may be correctable, as we discussed in Chapter 15. Urge him to have a routine eye and hearing exam—or make the appointments with him and accompany him to the doctors.

If he gets lost and is confused while driving in familiar territory, he may have a much more serious problem, the onset of dementia. You are sympathetic with his condition, of course. Like so many Americans, he is dependent on his car to get around, and without it he may feel isolated. On the other hand, if he has become dangerous behind the wheel, he could harm himself or others.

Brostoff suggests that you ask your father to go for a driving evaluation, which is available in many cities with comprehensive geriatric assessment programs. If he refuses, you can call his primary physician and report your concerns and ask the physician to send a report to the department of motor vehicles. Most states have a system for calling drivers in for a test under these circumstances. "Many people cease driving when they get a summons to be retested," notes Brostoff. There are also software packages that you can download into your computer; ask your dad to test his driving reflexes.

You may be concerned that you are liable for injuries or damage to property if you know your father was not driving safely but you failed to stop him. In case of an accident, your father would be the principal target of a suit, says Berg, an original founder of the National Academy of Elder Law Attorneys. You may be sued as well, but in most cases, the plaintiff would not win against you, notes Berg. However, you might feel excruciating moral anguish if your father hurt someone. Consider telling him how terrible he and the entire family would feel if that were to happen.

Louis's stepson wasn't willing to take a chance on such an eventuality. Louis insisted on driving at the age of ninety-two even though he became increasingly confused about where he was going while he was behind the wheel. Moreover, he continued to tailgate just as he did when he had the reflexes of a young man. His stepson, who didn't need an extra vehicle, borrowed Louis's car one day and kept "forgetting" to return it. Louis was furious and refused to speak to his stepson for the final few months of his life. But the stepson had the satisfaction of knowing he kept Louis safe and may have saved some lives.

Your Parents Refuse to Make a Will

For reasons we've talked about in Chapter 3 and will discuss again in Chapter 19, everyone should have a will. Those who fail to execute wills and companion documents like powers of attorney and advance directives with health care proxies leave their children frustrated and possibly fighting bitterly as well. What kind of medical care do Mom and Dad want at the ends of their lives? Do they want to be cremated? Who gets the car? Who gets mom's antique jewelry?

Seniors neglect to prepare such important documents for many reasons. Perhaps they don't want to go to the trouble and expense when they find out that a full set of documents, carefully prepared by a lawyer in a way that they all dovetail and cover all circumstances, can cost several thousand dollars. But inexpensive alternatives for at least some documents are available on the Internet and elsewhere.

As seniors' mental and physical health declines and the need for the advanced directives becomes even more imminent, an elderly couple may become more confused and feel more vulnerable and therefore be even less likely to attend to this task.

Jeff's father would be happy to prepare a will, but his mother, the dominant force in domestic decisions, will not hear of it. "She simply will not talk about anything that touches on death," says Jeff. It is not a matter of declining mental health as she gets older. She has avoided discussions of death all her life. Jeff, who is an editor, his sister, a doctor, and his brother, a lawyer, all try to reason with her, but she cannot be convinced.

Ultimately, after relatives and friends have made all their pleas to no avail, there is no legal or other recourse to force the couple to prepare a will. "The family may just have to accept that their parents will not make a decision," says Brostoff. "The siblings will just have to agree on some system of their own, perhaps even flipping a coin when two of them want the same item when the parents die without any direction to their children about how to divide up the estate."

Your Mother Is Suspicious of Strangers— and Even Caregivers

For seniors, almost any type of change can be very frightening. So don't be surprised if your mother is unreceptive to the idea of allowing a caregiver—most likely a stranger, at least in the beginning—into her home. In fact, this may be the first time that she's ever had help of any type in the house, so try to be patient and understanding of her attitude (especially if there are cognitive problems complicating the situation).

One possible means of dealing with your mother's resistance is to have her physician suggest that in-home help might be just the type of help she needs. Today's seniors are part of a generation that was inclined to follow "doctor's orders," so this approach could be particularly effective here.

Ease Her into It. And it also can help to make the introduction as comfortable as possible. Perhaps you could be involved in the initial meeting between your mother and her caregiver, or this meeting could be moderated by another representative from the caregiving agency—someone who can assure her that she's safe and will be well cared for.

However, if these approaches don't work and signs point to your mother being unable to adequately care for herself, then you might need to call the authorities. For instance, if there appear to be safety issues—or, in particular, if your mother seems to be engaging in self-neglect—then Adult Protective Services should be contacted (remember, though, that if she's of sound mind and body, these officials may be limited in their ability to intervene in your mother's affairs).

When Paranoia Points to Something More. Sometimes, however, the fear may become paranoia, which can be a symptom of Alzheimer's. If that's the case, acknowledge your mother's feelings and remain calm and understanding. When you communicate with her, don't argue. Instead, speak quietly and reassuringly, and focus entirely upon the conversation, making sure not to be distracted or preoccupied in any way.[1]

Remember that if your mother is exhibiting paranoia (or any other symptom) associated with Alzheimer's, she's not being deliberately difficult; it's just that her illness is interfering with her ability to determine and control her behaviors. While there currently is no known way to cure or prevent this disease, there are lifestyle and medication options that can help your mother maintain her mental function and manage her behavioral symptoms[2]—so make sure that her doctor remains updated on her medical and cognitive circumstances.

Your Mother Is Unmanageable at Home but Refuses to Go to a Nursing Home

Few people ever hoped they would spend their final days in a nursing home, and few children ever wanted to send their parents there. The hope of helping families avoid that option is in large part the reason we wrote this book. But sometimes there is no choice. Perhaps your mother is so disabled physically that she needs around-the-clock attendance. Maybe she is incontinent, refuses to take her medications, kicks and screams at her professional home caregivers, and has at times wandered out of the house in the middle of the night.

It is horrifying to see one's mother, once so gentle, loving, and rational, become hostile and physically combative. But such is the way advanced dementia can transform its victims. She is not acting that way out of willfulness. She cannot control her behavior.

Ask for an Assessment. The nursing home may be the only choice. But she won't go. "The first step is to hire a geriatric care manager and have an assessment made," says Berg. At the same time, consulting the website 4070talk.com will help you improve your communication skills with seniors. "Speak slowly," advises Berg. "Ask them to repeat what you said. Make sure you understand them and give them time. Seniors make decisions more slowly."

Explain to her that you will visit and evaluate several prospective homes. Ideally, the final decision on which home will be hers. You hope your mother will pick one in the community, but wherever she is, you will visit often. And if she doesn't like any of the options presented to her, then keep looking for other options.[3]

Last Resort. If she still refuses to go, however, you may have to resort to legal means, such as going to probate court and obtaining guardianship (which may take a significant amount of time). Generally, guardianship can be acquired over individuals who are incapable of making informed decisions. Such a legal relationship would afford you as the guardian the power to make decisions on your mother's behalf.[4]

More to the point, however, in a case such as this one, you would be able to preempt your mother's decision not to enter— or to leave—the nursing home (both of which are rights typically granted to those seniors of sound mind). However, do keep in mind that depending upon your home state, you may also have a legal obligation to communicate with your mother before making this or any other major decision.[5]

When You and Your Siblings Can't Agree

"Families come with a history," the Family Caregiver Alliance, caregiver.org, reminds us, "a history of how each person relates to the others, a history of what role each person has played and currently plays within the family, a history of how each person feels toward the person who is sick, and a history of how each person deals with illness and adversity. And in each family there are rules about what can and cannot be said, what emotions are okay and not okay to express."[6]

So when siblings gather to plan a strategy for dealing with the loved one in distress, there is a strong chance of significant disagreements among them. Generally, disagreements revolve around one or more of these issues:

■ Roles and rivalries dating back to childhood.
■ Disagreements over parents' conditions and capabilities.

- Disagreements over financial matters, which can influence decisions about where a parent should live, whether he can afford a housekeeper, and so forth. Arguments can be especially sharp when some siblings are better off financially than others.
- Burden of care. One sibling has to bear more responsibility for care than others, or at least feels she does.[7]

Concentrate on Practical Solutions for the Present

"One sibling can be unrealistic and believe that nothing is really wrong, and another can be alarmist and believe that the parent is in imminent danger when she is not," says Brostoff. "Also, families often take too long a time horizon—thinking that the immediate crisis they are facing will continue for years in the same form when usually it will change over time. What families need to concentrate on are practical solutions to the problem they are facing today."

Bring in Outside Help

To resolve conflicts among siblings, it is often helpful to invite to their gatherings a third-party facilitator who can stand apart from the family history and rivalries. A geriatric care manager can be such a facilitator, who not only can help identify all of the issues but also help the family understand what they have to focus on, and explain various alternatives.

You are not alone in having to consider the remedies, some agonizing, we have suggested in this chapter. As the population ages and until science comes up with cures for Alzheimer's and other dementia, more and more families will have to devise strategies, most of them emotionally painful to implement, to help loved ones in extreme distress.

Coping in a Strained Relationship

If you have had a difficult relationship with your mother or father all your life, unfortunately the chances are that it will only become more strained as you become his or her caregiver. "It's unlikely that old age and poor health will improve a personality that has always been critical, grumpy, intrusive, or just plain mean," observes Connie Matthiessen, senior editor of the website caring.com.[8] Still, you are a loving and dutiful child and want to help. Here are some of Matthiessen's suggestions for coping:

- **Talk it through.** Address the problem directly as soon as it arises. Use "I" statements when you explain your reactions. Instead of saying "You act like you hate me," try "I feel as if you are angry at me."
- **Prepare to have your buttons pushed.** Maybe your mother habitually compares you unfavorably to your siblings or blames you for a failed marriage. Get ready in advance for such a jibe—and quickly change the subject.
- **Try something different.** If sitting and talking with your mother generally leads to an argument, look for an alternative. Offer to weed her garden or cook her a special meal—something helpful that will also give both of you space.
- **Set boundaries.** If you're clear about how much you're willing and able to do for your father and stick to it, you'll be less susceptible to guilt trips and manipulative behavior. You can also set limits as to how much emotional abuse you'll put up with.[9]

17

Financing Care

Throughout the book as we have described options available to seniors, the focus has been on helping them find the setting that promotes their well-being, whether that be aging in place or assisted living or another alternative. Still, as we have talked about the costs of each alternative, you have likely come to a conclusion we fully appreciate: professional elder care is expensive, and it becomes more so at an accelerating rate as a senior's physical or mental health deteriorates.

Care Is Expensive!

The reason is clear. Caring for elders who have lost the ability to carry out their daily functions requires an enormous amount of time and labor. Currently there is no machinery that will lift your mother out of a bathtub or electronic device that will support your father as he learns to walk again. People do that demanding work, which is most of the reason that the charge for care in an assisted living facility averages $36,372 a year and the charge for a semiprivate room in a nursing home is about $70,000 a year.[1]

"There's a joke in which people ask why they should spend $5,000 a month in an assisted living facility when they could go instead on a cruise ship, travel the world, and get luxury room and board plus all their meals for that same $5,000 a month," observes Bill Comfort, owner of LTC insurance agency, Comfort Assurance Group. "But a cruise ship isn't going to help you get out of bed, get dressed, monitor your shower, or take you to and from your toilet. They're not going to cut up your steak and feed it to you. Neither is Holiday Inn."

Comfort's colorful story makes the point nicely. The big cost in care is not high-tech medical equipment, doctors' visits, or even hospital stays. Medicare covers most of those short-term expenses. The big cost is the ongoing everyday work trained professional caregivers perform in helping seniors through routines they used to manage effortlessly alone and providing the seniors with the companionship and encouragement to go on with their lives.

What Families Can Pay

As long as the senior remains relatively self-sufficient and there are family caregivers nearby to help, the cost of professional care-givers to supplement that care is probably manageable for most middle-class families on their usual incomes. On average, the services of a caregiver from Home Instead Senior Care, for exam-ple, cost about $18 an hour. Eight hours of help a week, which a typical Home Instead client purchases, is likely an amount many middle-class families can afford if they cut some expendable purchases elsewhere. Can you cut back on dinners out? Do you really need that second car?

But when the number of weekly hours climbs substantially, ordinary family budgets are overwhelmed. Ten hours a day, seven days a week of at-home nonmedical care, which someone with late-stage Alzheimer's or other advanced dementia might require, would be about the same cost as that of a nursing home, about $70,000 a year.

How can families possibly pay for such enormous costs? Should you, the family caregiver, and your siblings be responsible not only for hands-on care of your parents but pay for their profes-sional care as well? We can't answer that second question. Every family faces a different set of financial circumstances. How great are your resources? What other responsibilities do you have, such as your children's education, as well as your own future care? (We'll discuss your future care in Chapter 19.)

What Seniors Can Pay

What preparations have your parents made, not just for a healthy retirement, but also for an advanced age that likely will include some dependency? "Do you expect to live a long life? Do your parents? Of course, that's why you're so concerned about retire-ment savings and investment returns; even without the extra expense of care, running out of money is the greatest fear in retirement planning," Comfort asserts. "If you live to an advanced age, isn't it reasonable to assume you may need care for a period of years? That's why you need to understand the costs and need to have a plan."

Financing Alternatives

As forbidding as the financial challenges seem, millions of seniors do get excellent care in their final months and years, and your loved ones almost certainly will be among them. Generally, elder care is financed through a mix of the resources that follow.

Savings

Americans have been notoriously profligate in their spending in recent years and correspondingly neglectful of their savings. In a 2007 survey of retirees, Home Instead Senior Care discovered that two-thirds of those surveyed reported monthly incomes of less than $3,000 and assets of less than $75,000. Obviously, those resources will not pay for much home care or a long stay in a nursing home.

Let's assume that your parents have prospered in their working years and have been much thriftier than most. They plan to fund their own elder care and leave their financial estate intact to you and your siblings. That's an admirable objective, of course, but not easily achieved. In order to do so, they might need a portfolio of stocks, bonds, and other investments with a value of over $1 million. Here's the rough math we're using. A portfolio of $1 million would likely yield $50,000 or more a year, which would come close to the cost of assisted living, should your parents need it, and their estate would not be diminished.

Don't forget that if there's a spouse who must continue to live independently, there may be no way to allocate any income toward the costs of assisted living. Even well-to-do seniors risk their financial security when one spouse needs care while trying to maintain even a basic lifestyle for the independent spouse.

But suppose they have well less than $1 million and naively think that they can pay for a substantial amount of assisted living or nursing home or similar care without reducing their estate. The risk is that they will not set aside enough for themselves in order to leave you with an inheritance. "Families need to be very careful that they are making the best care decisions for their parents," advises Comfort, "not just the best decisions for the heirs financially."

Most seniors will not be able to finance their elder care entirely out of their savings. Still, elder care should have first call on those savings, and as much as grandpa or grandma would like to fund summer camp or vacations for the grandchildren, it may not be wise for them to do so.

Long-Term Care Insurance

This has become an increasingly popular way of funding elder care; some 8 million Americans are now covered by such policies, according to Home Instead Senior Care's *Long-Term-Care Insurance Resource Guide*. But as impressive as those numbers may seem, they are still dwarfed by the number of Americans who turn sixty-five every year and are thus within a few years of potentially needing such insurance. In 2011, the first wave of 2.7 million baby boomers will turn sixty-five, and each succeeding year the number will increase, peaking with 4.2 million new sixty-five-year-olds in 2025.[2]

Policies can be written in an almost endless variety of ways to provide a range of benefits from deluxe to frugal, covering all caregiver expenses for an unlimited amount of time or only partial expenses for a limited period. Buying such insurance is likely to demand much more thought than buying the more standard types of insurance you are accustomed to, such as life, auto, and homeowners. Consult a trusted insurance broker, financial advisor, or geriatric care manager, or better, all three. Make certain you understand what physical and medical condition you must be in before insurance begins to pay for your care.

How Much Care? Do you want insurance that will cover your care at home as well as in a nursing home, assisted care facility, or other setting? How much of the costs do you want the policy to cover? How will it complement the share of the costs you are able to pay out of savings and ordinary income? If your parents assume they will need twenty hours of professional care a week, they might want to cover half through long-term care insurance and half through savings. How long do they expect to need coverage?

A great drawback of long-term care insurance for many seniors is the high cost if they don't start buying it until late in life. Initiated when the policyholder is at the age of seventy, an average policy can cost $4,000 a year, according to Comfort's calculations based on rates of the four largest insurers.

"Shared Benefits" Option. But your parents don't have to buy full coverage. Here's one possible scenario involving two policies, one for your mother and another for your father. Let's assume that she is sixty-five and he is sixty-nine. She is likely to live for many more years than he does, both because she is younger and because women tend to live longer than men.

So it is possible to imagine that at some point your father is going to decline first and need care. But your mother will still be in good health and able to provide most of that care. What she needs is a professional caregiver to come in three days a week for two hours to stay with your father so that she can shop, watch her grandchildren's school play, and so forth.

By the time your mother begins to decline, she may be a widow, living alone. You and your siblings are perhaps far away or have jobs that take up your days. So your mother might need twelve hours of professional care a week, twice as much as your father did, and, eventually, coverage for assisted living or a nursing home.

While buying a shorter policy on Dad, say two years, and a longer one on Mom, for four years, appears to make sense, it doesn't provide any flexibility if the circumstances end up being different. A newer feature called "shared benefits" allows a couple to combine their policies into a single shared benefit—in our example, it would be for a total of six years. The policy can then be used in any combination, for the first care need if longer than expected, or all of the unused benefits can be rolled over to the surviving spouse to use later.

Again, buying long-term care insurance is a lot more complicated than homeowners' insurance. Consult advisors and the organizations listed at the end of this chapter.

Reverse Mortgage

A relatively new source of income that seniors, in this case those over sixty-two years of age, increasingly rely on is the reverse mortgage. The Federal Trade Commission website, ftc.gov (search for "reverse mortgages"), and other sources listed at the end of the chapter provide a detailed explanation of how a reverse mortgage works, but here's a short version. Assume that your parents have paid off the mortgage on their house and that it has a market value of $500,000. They might enter into an agreement by which the bank would in effect pay them an income-tax-free mortgage, $2,000 a month, say. Your parents would be allowed to remain in the home as long as they lived or chose to stay. They would have to continue to pay real estate taxes on their home and also the upkeep, including major repairs.

If one of your parents dies, the survivor would be able to continue living in the house until he or she died, or perhaps moved to a nursing home. At that point, the estate would pay the bank the cash the owners have received, plus interest and fees. If the heirs sell the house to pay the bank, they keep the rest of the proceeds.[3] Obviously, a reverse mortgage is a major and complex commitment that could have considerable consequences for the entire family. Your parents should not enter into such an agreement without the advice of an attorney and financial planner.

Life Settlement

Another recent senior care funding innovation you may want to consider is the "life settlement" in which the senior's life insurance policy is treated as an asset in the same way that a house, mutual fund, or even a sports car collection are assets. With a life settlement, the senior's life insurance policy is sold to an investor while the policy holder is still alive for considerably more than the cash surrender value of the policy but far less than its face value. At the time of the sale, your father will receive a lump sum payment—expect less than half the face value of the policy depending upon his age, health, and other factors. The investor will continue to make the premium payments for your father's policy and finally collect its full face value after your father's demise.

Life settlements may provide quick access to much needed resources for your senior, but be aware that the investors buying your father's life insurance policy stand to profit considerably on the proceeds of the policy. However, the overriding consideration is what's best for him.

You should also be aware that many life settlement organizations have relationships with senior care businesses including care facilities. While this may be convenient, it also requires extra diligence. Because of the many complexities involving life settlements, we strongly encourage you to consult with financial advisors before taking this step.

Medicare

This is a federal health insurance program that covers almost all Americans over the age of sixty-five for a large share of their medical expenses, such as hospitalization, doctor bills, x-rays, radiation, and a great variety of other tests and therapies. The senior generally has to make a co-payment for a part of those expenses, although many seniors have privately funded so-called medigap policies to supplement Medicare. For example, Medicare requires the patient to pay a large deductible ($1,000 and up) when admitted to a hospital and a 20 percent co-payment for all outpatient and doctors' services. But a medigap policy might pay for those out-of-pocket costs associated with Medicare-approved expenses.

Medicare, moreover, does not pay for nonmedical care, including the long-term care and assistance with daily living activities that we are concerned with in this chapter.[4] Comfort also points out that it does not pay for long-term-care room and board anywhere—at home, in an assisted living community, or in a nursing home. However, he notes that there are a few important exceptions to the rule for the last arrangement. For instance, Medicare will pay up to a maximum of 100 days of a stay in a nursing home, fully for the first 20 days and partially for the next 80 days (as described in Chapter 11). The payments continue only as long as the senior is in a skilled rehabilitative program, perhaps learning once again to walk or groom herself. Once the rehab is no longer effective in improving the senior's condition or abilities, Medicare stops paying, even if this happens in less than 100 days.

After that period, at least as Medicare views it, a stay in a nursing home is custodial. If, however, while your mother is in the nursing home, she has a stroke or has to be taken to an acute care hospital for some other emergency, Medicare will pay, just as it would do if she were not in a nursing home. Medicare will also pay for rehabilitation therapy and limited care visits at home, but again only if the skilled therapy is improving the senior's condition. Also, Medicare will pay for nonmedical services once a senior has entered hospice care (as described in Chapter 12).

Medicare Advantage

A newer alternative for seniors is a Medicare Advantage plan. This is a private-insurance alternative to traditional Medicare's deductible and co-payment system and does not require a medigap policy. Seniors continue to pay their Medicare Part B premiums, but if they enroll in a Medicare Advantage plan, those premiums are passed on to the private insurer along with an annual payment for Part A inpatient costs. The Medicare Advantage plan then agrees to manage the senior's care within those funding limits. Medicare Advantage plans are private medical insurance with a network of preferred providers and per visit co-payments for doctors' visits and hospitalization. Some Medicare Advantage plans have a small monthly premium, but typically much less than a medigap premium. While Medicare Advantage plans can add services not typically covered by Medicare—like annual physicals and other preventive services—none of them provide any custodial long-term care coverage beyond Medicare's skilled, rehabilitative services already noted.

Medicaid

This is a program often confused with Medicare because they are both health care programs. But Medicaid is a "means tested" welfare program designed to help the poor of all ages, including the elderly. For those under sixty-five, Medicaid generally pays for medical costs, such as maternity bills for poor women and pediatric care for their children. For those over sixty-five, it will help pay for their nursing home costs once they have exhausted all, or almost all, of their own means. Medicaid generally will only pay for care in a certified nursing home. Some states offer very limited home care benefits under Medicaid, but the time and scope of home care services is very limited.

Medicaid is administered by the individual states (it is called Medi-Cal in California), and therefore the rules for qualifying vary somewhat from state to state.[5] Check the government website govbenefits.gov and then select "Medicaid/Medicare" for the rules in your state. Also, consult a geriatric care manager or elder care attorney on state rules.

When Medicaid Helps. Typically, Medicaid eligibility comes into play in a situation like the following, which we described in somewhat greater detail in Chapter 11. Your mother suffers a stroke and is taken to an acute care hospital. A week later her condition is stable, but you cannot care for her at home. The hospital helps you find her a place in a nursing home. The nursing home fee is, say, $6,000 a month. If your mother has $60,000 in assets, the family will have to "spend down" those assets for nine months or so until she has only about $2,000 left.

For single people, the house may have to be sold with the proceeds becoming part of the spend-down assets. Not every state enforces this at the time of eligibility. But many states now require payback of care costs from home equity after the death of the Medicaid beneficiary. This is what is called "estate recovery." For couples in which one spouse—whom Medicaid calls the "community spouse"—is still living in the home, the home is protected as long as he or she is living there. The community spouse can also keep one-half of the couple's other assets, but only up to a maximum of just over $100,000. Note that these "non-countable" assets may still be at risk of confiscation by Medicaid after the death of the community spouse. Check with an elder-law attorney or Medicare/Medicaid expert on current guidelines.

Federal and state Medicaid laws have changed in recent years to severely restrict and penalize any efforts by seniors or their families to "artificially impoverish" a senior by giving away or spending down the senior's assets in order to qualify for Medicaid.

Once your mother is in a nursing home, you and your mother, with the help of the nursing home, will apply for Medicaid. Your mother will almost certainly qualify, as long as she can establish she has few assets left. Most likely, she will stay in the same nursing home; her care will be the same as when she was a paying resident if the nursing home has Medicaid-certified beds. Then Medicaid will help pay her bills.

Finally, Medicaid not only requires a senior to deplete her assets, but once she qualifies for Medicaid, she has to pay any remaining monthly income, such as social security or a pension check, to the nursing home. Medicaid only pays the difference between the senior's remaining income and the nursing home's monthly charge.

Future of Medicaid. The necessity of impoverishing your mother to have her cared for in her final months or years may very well be painful to your family, as it is to other families. But with no alternatives, an enormous number of families do just that. Of the 1.6 million seniors in nursing homes today, two-thirds of them are on Medicaid.[6]

Whether Medicaid can go on paying those costs indefinitely is one of the critical policy questions of the day. It is hard to imagine how Medicaid can do so without somehow reducing its contribution. Stephen A. Moses, president of the Center for Long-Term Care Reform, notes that on average about one-quarter of total state budgets is now dedicated to paying Medicaid expenses.

That spending includes medical care for those indigent women and children we mentioned earlier. But between one-third and one-half of the Medicaid budget goes to elderly people in nursing homes. As aging baby boomers enter nursing homes in the coming years, they will add to those costs at an accelerating rate.

If your mother or father enters a nursing home in the near future, he or she will likely qualify for Medicaid once he or she has spent the assets of a lifetime.

Financing Resources

- AARP, aarp.org
- Access America for Seniors, seniors.gov
- AgingCare.com
- CaregiverList.com
- Federal Trade Commission, ftc.gov (search for "reverse mortgages")
- HelpGuide.org (search for "payment options")
- U.S. Department of Housing and Urban Development (HUD), hud.gov
- Medicare website, medicare.gov
- MetLife Mature Market Institute, metlife.com/mmi
- National Academy of Elder Law Attorneys, naela.org
- National Senior Citizens Law Center, nsclc.org

18

Don't Forget Yourself

We're going to shift focus in this chapter in order to make you, the caregiver, the center of attention. To the extent that it's possible for anyone to step outside herself, we ask you to do just that. Make as analytical and as loving an appraisal of yourself as you have made of your loved one. Try to look at yourself as though you were a third person and ask yourself, What are the caregiver's needs? What family support, what professional help, what daily routines and disciplines does the caregiver need to get through this period that is very demanding and stressful on the caregiver, no matter how rewarding it might be?

Who Cares for the Caregiver?

Taking care of your loved one can have an enormous impact on your health and well-being. (See "How Stressed Are You?" box in this chapter.) The responsibility can take a serious toll on you even if other family members are sharing the burden. So be aware of these danger signs that indicate you might be close to your breaking point and have to step back a little or find an additional source of strength, perhaps through counseling: persistent anxiety and irritability, sleeplessness, frequent headaches or illnesses, or even noticeable strain on family relationships.

Your caregiving mission is not a success if your loved one becomes stabilized and plateaus to a long and reasonably healthy old age and you become sick and disabled in the process. Obviously, a damaged caregiver is less effective than a whole one. But more than that, although the principal concern throughout this book has been with the failing senior, an overriding interest is the health and well-being of the entire family.

Few of us who are either currently family caregivers or will be someday are ideal for the assignment. Yes, we are loving and devoted to the senior we are taking care of and take great pleasure in being able to help at the end of their lives the mothers and fathers who raised us. Yes, we are competent and responsible adults.

That's all to the good. But as family caregivers, we have serious handicaps as well. Many of us have full-time careers that can't be suspended while we are caring for our loved ones. Even when we are exhausted after a hard day at the office, we can't put aside the care of the senior dependent on us. Also, we have spouses and children who understandably expect our attention as well, and competition for the attention we are paying a needy senior can cause considerable stress.

Protect Other Relationships

"You have to figure out how to be a caregiver without letting your relationship with your children and spouse suffer," advises Keren Brown-Wilson, a professor at Portland State University's Institute on Aging. We used her guidance a good deal in preparing this chapter. "This is a point of contention in many marriages where couples have to provide care for the parents of one spouse." Your husband may love your father, but that won't necessarily stop him from feeling jealous if you're spending all your time with Dad.

Also, you, the caregiver, generally have a long and complicated, although loving, history with the person you are caring for. That can lead you to personalize problems and notch up the level of stress. You may have different expectations of him than you would of someone you are not related to.

If you were taking care of a stranger and the stranger were incontinent, it might be unpleasant to deal with, but you wouldn't take it as an insult. If your parent is incontinent, you might blurt out in irrational anger, "Why are you doing this to me? Just because I'm your daughter, it doesn't mean you can make me take care of messes like this." Observes Brown-Wilson: "It is important to recognize that our emotional involvement can make it more difficult to do a good job of caregiving."

Doing Too Much

Finally, you are likely trying to do too much by yourself. According to a national survey by Home Instead Senior Care, three out of four caregivers do the job by themselves without help from other family members, friends, or professionals.

How Stressed Are You?

If you feel persistent anxiety or stress in your role as caregiver, be assured that you are not alone. In a survey of 16,000 caregivers, Home Instead Senior Care discovered that many share your views. The numbers in the right-hand column represent the percentage of people agreeing or strongly agreeing with the statements on the left.

I'm feeling anxious or irritable.	88%
I'm feeling overwhelmed by the caregiving role.	75%
I'm seeing a toll on family relationships.	74%
I'm experiencing disturbed sleep patterns.	72%
I'm feeling "stressed out."	72%
I'm experiencing more frequent illness/headaches.	54%
I'm feeling resentment toward the person cared for.	43%
I'm feeling financial strain on self/family.	38%

To take a measure of your own stress levels, we invite you to visit Caregiverstress.com, where you can take your own assessment and receive advice about where to find resources to help.

As stresses build one upon another, you lose your ability to help your loved one as you grow angrier about your situation and often angry at your loved one for a condition he or she has no control over. "The physical work is hard," says Brown-Wilson, "but the emotional work is harder." For example, a recent study found that one-third of family caregivers for people with dementia showed signs of depression.[1]

Especially if you are middle-aged and taking care of both ailing parents and adolescent children, you face an increased risk of depression, chronic illness, and a possible decline in the quality of your life. As the senior's mental and physical health declines, your health is challenged as well. What can you do to reduce the stress on yourself?

Get Others to Help

If you are the primary caregiver, make it clear to others that if you have to do the job all alone, over time you may break down (and possibly drop responsibility for Mom altogether). We recognize that in some circumstances it is extremely difficult to get family and friends to lend a hand. Your aunts live far away. Your siblings are overwhelmed by other family or business problems.

But sometimes the family caregiver is simply not being assertive enough about her needs. In fact, the primary caregiver should have the most significant voice in discussions about providing care for senior loved ones—including being able to ask for help from other family members. (This assumes, of course, that the primary caregiver is constructively providing care and/or guiding the delivery of care and is not unnecessarily complicating the care process.)

Often, of course, the lack of support is the fault of other siblings, who use excuses like distance or clumsiness to evade responsibility. "A sibling living far away has all sorts of misconceptions about the caregiving," notes Brown-Wilson. "The primary caregiver should suggest to this sibling that he or she do some of the caregiving in order to understand what the situation is." If the sibling comes and stays with Mom for a week, the visit will have the additional benefit of giving the primary caregiver much-needed time off.

Your Brother's Help

Perhaps your brother feels incapable of cleaning the house well or is embarrassed by the prospect of helping your mother bathe. That's understandable, and you don't want to force someone to help. "It's really important not to be critical of people who are not suited to caregiving," Brown-Wilson counsels, "because that's when elder abuse happens." Instead, have your brother pay for professionals to come in and help out for a few hours a week.

Enlist your mother's neighbors in the effort. Knock on Mrs. Johnson's door and tell her that you would like to bring her up to date on your mother's condition. In the course of the chat, you can mention that it would be great if Mrs. Johnson could stop in and help Mom make breakfast every Tuesday when you have an early morning meeting.

Payback Time

If Mrs. Johnson seems resistant to helping, drop somewhere in the conversation your memories of how fond Mom is of Mrs. Johnson and how much she enjoyed feeding Mrs. Johnson's cat when Mrs. Johnson was away. Perhaps it's not in your nature to be overbearing, but don't hesitate to be a little persistent about payback time.

Many caregivers grope for the communication skills to get support. It's not easy, but try to develop a procedure, a couple of key phrases, perhaps, that you are comfortable with and enable you to ask for help. For example, a colleague has developed a simple, inexpensive, yet ingenious device. She writes down her needs on separate 4″ × 4″ cards—"grocery shopping" on one card, for example, "shovel driveway" on another, and "fill out insurance forms" on a third. Whenever someone asks how he can help, she hands him an appropriate card.

Protect Your Body and Mind

Surveys indicate that caregivers are less likely than noncaregivers to practice preventive self-care, including health care. They report that they have problems attending to their own health and well-being while taking care of someone else.[2]

Exercise is a great antidote to stress. If you're not already an accomplished tennis player, the chances are that you are not going to undertake learning a sport like tennis while trying to work caregiving into your schedule. But you don't have to do anything as demanding as tennis or jogging or even swimming.

That doesn't mean you can't find ways to take care of yourself while taking care of Mom. For example, take your mother to her doctor's appointment, and while she is in his office, walk up and down the stairs of the medical building. If you feel embarrassed about doing this, explain to your mother's doctor what you're doing. He'll probably prescribe it to all caregivers. Form a partnership with your mom's physician that addresses your health needs as well as those of your loved one.[3] It's important that your well-being—and limitations—are taken into account to ensure your loved one gets the best care.

Get a Checkup

While you are in the medical building, make an appointment for an annual checkup for yourself, a routine that family caregivers are inclined to neglect. Eat well, including plenty of fresh fruits, vegetables, nuts, beans, and whole grains. Go easy on caffeine,

Eight Ways to Help Yourself

Most family caregivers struggle to balance care for an aging parent or relative with other major responsibilities. This often means that there is little time to care for themselves, which can result in poor health and high levels of stress. Below are some tips for avoiding and managing caregiver stress from the experts on the Home Instead Senior Care Advisory Board:

- **Work out.** Exercise and enjoy something you like to do (walking, dancing, biking, running, swimming, etc.) for a minimum of twenty minutes at least three times per week. Yoga and Tai Chi teach inner balance and relaxation.
- **Meditate.** Sit still and breathe deeply with your mind as quiet as possible whenever things feel like they are moving too quickly or you are feeling overwhelmed.
- **Ask for help.** According to a national survey by Home Instead Senior Care of adults who are currently providing care for an aging loved one, 72 percent do so without any outside help. Reach out to others for aid.
- **Take a break.** Make arrangements for reliable fill-in help (family, friends, volunteers, or professional caregivers) and take single days or even a week's vacation. When you're away, stay away. Talk about everything but caregiving; read that book you haven't been able to get to.
- **Eat well.** Eat plenty of fresh fruits, vegetables, and proteins, including nuts, beans, and whole grains.
- **Take care of yourself.** Just as you make sure your loved one gets to the doctor, make sure you get your annual checkup. Being a caregiver provides many excuses for skipping many chores. Don't skip your checkups.
- **Indulge.** Treat yourself to a foot massage or manicure; take a walk, rent a movie, have a nice dinner out, or take

> in a concert to take yourself away from the situation
> and to reward yourself for the wonderful care you are
> providing to your aging relative.
>
> - **Support.** Find a local caregiver support group that will
>   help you understand that what you are feeling is normal
>   for someone in your position. This is also an organization
>   to go to for practical advice on day-to-day challenges.

fast food, and sweets—which will provide a quick "pick-me-up" followed by an equally rapid letdown.

Also, find a local caregiver support group, such as the Caregiver Alliance, or a similar organization. Not only will members of the group have practical advice for dealing with day-to-day problems, but simply meeting others in a situation like your own will give you a feeling of community, an assurance that you are not alone. In addition, pick a good friend or friends you can telephone anytime you need morale building or to let off steam.

Confront Your Emotions

Sometimes caregivers experience stress because they have unrealistic expectations about the outcome of their mission (yet, conversely, at other times, they may not even recognize what they're doing constitutes caregiving). They get frustrated or angry because they think they should be able to provide more or better care. Or they feel lonely because of the effects that caregiving has had on their social lives. But research indicates that people who take an active role in dealing with caregiving issues (and solving related problems) are less likely to feel stressed than those who simply worry or feel helpless.[4]

So you might ask yourself some of these questions: Do you feel you have to be the "perfect" caregiver? What (and how good) is the nature of the relationship with the person to whom you're providing care? Are you reluctant to ask others for help—whether it be with actual caregiving tasks, or, for instance, finances? Are you willing to say "no" to requests that prove draining when added to your caregiving burden (such as preparing holiday meals)? These are the kinds of questions that we should ask ourselves. You can bring them up with members of your support group and find out how others deal with them.[5]

Set Boundaries on Demands

One common problem for family caregivers is the parent in an assisted living facility or nursing home who wants a high level of attention the facility doesn't offer. Or she might complain that the professional caregiver who comes to her home doesn't cook the way you do or iron her dresses correctly. She wants you to iron and cook for her. "It is very difficult for the caregiver to manage all the wants and needs and still have her own life," observes Brown-Wilson.

To cope with such requests, says Brown-Wilson, you, the caregiver, must have a clear idea in your mind of your mother's routine and determine what you are able to do for her and what others must do. Prioritize what is most important to her. Tell her what you cannot do for her and tell her why. "Mom, I can't cook for you because I work late and have to make dinner for the children." Always explain why you can't do something, says Brown-Wilson, because if you don't, she will bring up the request again and again.

Be Forthright

But negotiate as well. Even though you can't cook dinner for her every night, invite her to your home on Sundays or promise you will take her out to dinner. If she is obstinate on an issue, tell her she is forcing you to tell her what cannot be done rather than helping you work out a compromise. "The trick is to be as positively forthright as possible," says Brown-Wilson.

In this chapter we have looked at you and your needs as caregiver. In the next and final chapter, we will consider you in another role: the reflective and responsible middle-aged adult anticipating and planning for the time you will no longer be the caregiver, but the care recipient.

Planning Your Own Future

N ow we turn our attention entirely to you, the caregiver. As you have read this book, you have certainly reflected often on the time when you might be no longer the caregiver but the care recipient. Will you be crippled by osteoporosis like your mother? Will it be your destiny to fade into dementia at the age of eighty as your father did? Or will you have a healthy old age and go quickly? None of us knows for sure, so some planning is a good idea.

So we ask you to take an inventory of all of your resources, just as you took inventory of your parents' resources in earlier chapters. Who is likely to be your primary family caregiver? Who can he or she count on for support? How about your emotional and spiritual resources? You have been physically active all your life. Suppose you were confined to a wheelchair? Or, what if you were no longer able to read? How would you cope with such limitations? Who is the clergyman, best friend, child, sibling you would turn to for advice and solace? And what are your financial resources for dealing with a possible collapse of your physical or mental health?

Remarkable Senior Performances

We live in an invigorating, promising, and yet somewhat contradictory era in which large numbers of seniors are healthier than seniors have ever been. They play singles tennis, climb mountains, ride in motorcycle rallies, ski expert runs, race bicycles, and swim remarkable distances. Former president George H. W. Bush celebrated his eightieth birthday by parachuting out of a plane onto the grounds of his presidential library.

The median life expectancy of an American man of sixty-five is now seventeen more years and a few months. The life expectancy of a sixty-five-year-old woman is twenty more years.[1] But although those seniors may live longer than their predecessors, many will lead lives in which they will likely experience more physical and medical issues than those who went before. Half of middle-aged adults between fifty-five and sixty-four have high blood pressure.[2] Almost one in five Americans over the age of sixty has diabetes.[3]

If present trends continue, many more American adults likely will be overweight or obese in the coming decades. Moreover, experts believe that along with being prone to the aforementioned diseases, these individuals may have an increased risk of developing functional disabilities[4]—in other words, an inability to perform those daily activities that help us stay independent, safe, and happy.

Heredity and Lifestyle Matter

So although all of us hope to live until we are ninety-five and then have a quick end on the tennis court or at some other favorite venue, the odds are that we will not. The good news, however, is that most of us will not be condemned to decades of misery either. "There are only two pictures of older people, those who are frail and helpless or those who are vital and healthy," says Dr. Keren Brown-Wilson, a professor in the Institute on Aging at Portland State University. "But the truth of the matter is that there is a bell curve, with a few people at either extreme and the rest in the middle."

Where you will end up on the curve and how much care, if any, you will need depend on a number of variables. Heredity can be a predictor of your future. If one of your parents suffers from Alzheimer's disease, for example, you may have a greater chance of doing the same.[5] Diet and exercise are major factors, as we discussed in the previous chapter; women are more likely than men to need care, because they tend to live longer; and single people often require more paid care because they have fewer family members to help out. And luck, of course, will be a considerable and unpredictable force in determining your final years.

Shoot for the Galapagos but Prepare for the Worst

How should you prepare yourself for a future that on the one hand promises long and robust health but on the other threatens a steady decline into frailty and dependence?

By all means plan for a comfortable, exciting retirement in which you realize the lifelong dream of a trip to the Galapagos Islands or the Taj Mahal, or simply spending day after day fishing, golfing, and taking grandchildren to the playground.

But plan simultaneously for the time when that wonderful retirement might be cut short, gradually or suddenly, by accident or disease. Any of us could spend months, or perhaps years, with our physical or mental aptitudes in disheartening decline.

Prepare Now

And you should begin to plan immediately, because as you likely know from the experience with your parents that brought you to this book to begin with, if you wait for an emergency to begin planning, the emotional and financial difficulties will be multiplied. You owe it to both yourself and to your family to begin to prepare now.

Prioritize

Think sensibly about the basic needs in your life, beyond food and other essentials, and focus on what you could give up and could not give up. Perhaps you can eventually sell your twenty-foot fishing boat, which spends most of the time at the marina anyhow, but the winter trip to Florida will remain high on your list of priorities.

Buy a Home to Last

If you are moving, either within your current area or many miles away, contemplate the kind of house you will want not just next year, but in ten or fifteen years, when you are likely to be less enthusiastic about climbing flights of stairs. Also, return to Chapter 4, "Aging in Place," in which we explain the alterations and modifications that are helpful to everyone but essential for many seniors, among them grab bars in showers, good lighting, wide front doors to accommodate wheelchairs, and a ramp alongside the front steps.

Perhaps you are looking for a house with five bedrooms to accommodate all the grandkids because you have persuaded yourself that all of them will come visit you often. Be realistic. They may come separately, but all of them will descend on you en masse once a year, at most, unless you live in a ski lodge or a beach house. Get a smaller house with two bedrooms. When the entire crowd of grandkids arrives on that once-a-year occasion, rent suites of rooms at the best hotel in town, which is a much cheaper way to house them, and you can put the money you save by buying a smaller house into an emergency fund.

Estate Planning

Everyone, and certainly everyone with children, should have a formal, comprehensive, in-writing estate plan that designates a power of attorney for someone else to act in their behalf should they become incapacitated; that sets out their wishes for medical treatment at the end of life; that designates a health care proxy when they can no longer make choices on their own; and explains how they want their material estate distributed upon death. You will likely need an attorney for at least some of these procedures.

Will

You can't assume that your children or other heirs are going to apportion whatever money you leave in a way that you would consider fair. Your daughter with children to be educated might conclude, legitimately in her mind, that she is entitled to most of the money and your childless son to very little. Make your wishes clear and legal in a will. Even when the financial consequences of dying without a will are small, the emotional repercussions can be tremendous. When you die, who is going to get the furniture that you and your spouse made with your own hands? And what are you going to do for those who don't get the furniture?

If you have minor children, you will want to designate guardians for them. Obviously, you'll tell the proposed guardians in advance of your wishes. Maybe you have chosen the guardians because their lifestyles are much like your own so that, hopefully, the transition would be much easier for the children. Explain to other members of the family why you have chosen as you have and make it clear that even though they will not be the legal guardians, you want them to play important roles in your children's lives as well.

Advance Directive

This document is as crucial as a will (and is sometimes referred to as a living will) and emotionally might be even more difficult to face. The document states your wishes in case some terrible accident or medical episode leaves you near death with little or no chance of recovery. Do you want artificial feeding and respiration? Or do you decline any attention other than liquids and pain relievers? Or something in-between?

Talk this over with your doctor before you complete the directive and ask him to explain procedures that may seem confusing (remembering that even some physicians are uncomfortable talking about end-of-life issues).[6] Once you have completed the directive, make sure your physician gets a copy. Every U.S. state has a law about completing advance directives, and these laws also require health care providers to honor these directives.[7]

The same document, or an additional one, creates a health care proxy, a relative or friend who can make decisions about retaining doctors, say, or moving you to another hospital or helping the hospital staff interpret any ambiguities in the advance directive.

Technically, your proxy (or "agent") has the legal right to make decisions for you if you can no longer speak for yourself. However, if close family members disagree or argue with the proxy about your course of treatment, your doctor may find it difficult to honor your wishes. So, by documenting your intentions in an advance directive, you're not only making sure the treatment team knows specifically what you want done (or not done), but you're also helping your proxy actually carry out your plan.[8]

So to help avoid these types of disagreements from arising, start by talking with family members, friends, and spiritual advisors to clarify that type of care that's meaningful and important to you. Make sure they know you have an advance directive, and provide copies to each. Finally, let them know as and when you make changes to this document (it's a good idea to review advance directives at least annually and to make appropriate modifications as your personal situation changes).[9]

Power of Attorney

You should give someone the power of attorney to act on your behalf if you are disabled in an accident or by an illness. Even though you will likely recover to take care of your own finances and sign important papers, in the meantime someone will have to sign the papers for the mortgage refinancing or the lease on the summer cabin. Your spouse is the obvious choice to have your power of attorney, but she might also be the person likeliest to be sitting next to you in a car accident. So give your power of attorney to an alternate as well.

Last Wishes

While your family knows you well and will want to provide an end chapter to your life consistent with your wishes, you can do them a great favor by providing final instructions that address the following questions and other issues that are important to you. How do you want your remains disposed of? Do you want a traditional funeral and burial, or cremation? Do you have special requests for a service? Again, these are unsettling questions to have to answer, but don't put the burden of making these decisions on your children. Having gone through your parents' deaths, you may know how painful and divisive such decisions can be for families.

The Future of Financing Care

We talk about financing care in detail in Chapter 17, and our advice on savings and reverse mortgages applies to you as it did to your parents. Whether you choose to arrange a reverse mortgage or not, one way or another you may well have to use your equity in your home, either through another form of loan or by selling it, to help pay for your care in the final stages of your life. As a result, the tradition of parents handing down their homes to their children as an inheritance may end for many families.

An enormous question—and for now an unanswerable one— is what role government will continue to play in the medical and nonmedical care of seniors, including those who are physically or mentally impaired. For almost all of those above sixty-five, the federal Medicare program pays most doctor fees, hospital bills, and prescription drugs. Although it is a very expensive program

($431 billion in fiscal year 2007),[10] it is also an extremely popular one and not likely to be curtailed seriously.

Will Medicaid Survive?

Less secure is Medicaid, a nationwide program administered by the individual states and financed by them along with the federal government. Medicaid supports health care for the poor of all ages. In the case of seniors it supports mostly those who have exhausted their private resources during stays in nursing homes. They have no means other than Medicaid to pay for their nursing-home room and board, the comfort and companionship of professional caregivers, or help with the classic six activities of daily living: dressing, bathing, eating, moving from one place to another, toileting, and staying continent.

So many nursing home residents have used up their own funds and joined the rolls of Medicaid that they are overwhelming the ability of the states to support them (in fact, for 2007, total Medicaid spending in the United States exceeded $329 billion, more than a 6 percent increase relative to 2006).[11] Typically, Medicaid payments consume some 20 percent or more of a state's entire budget,[12] which includes schools, highways, social services, police, and all other expenses. That flow of dollars to recipient programs—including long-term care options such as nursing homes—cannot go on, argues Stephen A. Moses, president of the Center for Long-Term Care Reform.

Long-Term Care Protection

"If you are looking at long-term care through the rearview mirror, what you see is that Mom and Dad or Grandma and Grandpa got their nursing home care paid for by Medicaid," says Moses. "It isn't going to continue, so you better start looking ahead through the windshield at what's coming. And if you do that, what you'll see is the brick wall of fiscal reality coming at you at 100 miles an hour."

How can you protect yourself from the collision that Moses envisions? One way is to reinforce the income you expect from savings and the equity in your home with long-term care insurance. We describe this insurance in Chapter 17, but we repeat it here, because fifty is a more appropriate age to start thinking about such insurance than is seventy. "You can buy long-term care insurance at sixty or seventy, but the numbers show the value of buying it earlier in your life," says Bill Comfort of Comfort Assurance Group. "So we typically suggest that people start looking at long term care insurance at fifty and purchase it by fifty-five."

A typical policy purchased currently would provide $100 a day worth of care, roughly the cost of a professional nonmedical caregiver at home for five hours a day at current rates. A reassuring policy would cover you for four years of care with a provision for inflation of 5 percent a year compounded. In other words, next year the policy would pay $105 a day and the year after, $110.25 a day, and so on.

Advantage of Buying Early. For a fifty-year-old in good health, the cost of such a policy offered by four major insurance companies today averages about $1,750 a year, with no increase in the premiums as times goes on. For a seventy-year-old in good health, the cost averages about $4,035 a year, which demonstrates the advantage of buying a policy at a younger age.

Consider a "Shared Benefit" Policy. This is not the only choice of policies available. As we pointed out in Chapter 17, if you are an older male and your wife is younger, you may determine that you can take a chance on a less generous policy for yourself, only two years of care for you, for example, and four years of care for her; because she will likely remain in good health for a long time after you begin to decline, she can provide much of your care herself.

We believe that if you take the time and make the effort to get ready for the final stages of your life, as difficult and as expensive as some of those preparations may be, you will make that part of your life far more secure and fulfilling than it would otherwise be for both you and your loved ones.

Afterword

As advocates for seniors around the world, we want to thank you for taking steps to educate yourself about the care options available to your older loved ones. The care journey you are on—or are preparing for—will likely become one of the most challenging and rewarding journeys you will undertake. Having been down this path with our own families and observing it in thousands of others, we know the road can seem dark, steep, crooked, and—possibly—never ending. There are so many avenues for seniors and their loved ones to take. The more information you have at your fingertips, the better equipped you will be to make the best decisions.

As a caregiver to your parents, aging family members, or friends, you have been granted the awesome privilege of helping some of our most vulnerable people in their greatest time of need and dependence. You have an extraordinary opportunity to help your seniors maintain independence, dignity, and self-respect by leading them through the maze of choices available. We think this is one of the higher callings in life and hope that through this book we've offered you guidance and opened doors to a more satisfying future for you and your family. We also hope you take comfort in knowing that you are not on this path alone.

Through our personal journey caring for aging family members, we found that the hills and valleys were eased considerably by our strong faith in God. When moments seemed the darkest, we turned to our faith for comfort, guidance, and peace. Genuine sustaining faith provides courage, strength, endurance, and joy in the midst of even the greatest difficulty.

As a caregiver, you will face situations that seem more than you are able to bear. Perhaps that's your situation now. If it is, we would like to offer encouragement that faith does not disappoint. Faith has made all the difference in our lives and how we face trials—even if it doesn't change our circumstances. When God gave us the Fifth Commandment—"Honor your father and your mother"—He made evident his love for seniors. By learning about and providing the best care for the seniors in your life, you are living God's commandment every day.

Faith can take very different forms. In our home, faith in God is paramount. Some find strength in religious beliefs that are very different from ours. Others may find comfort and peace in nature, in family traditions, or in other forms of emotional and spiritual support. Take refuge in your beliefs and remember that grace and dignity come in many forms and can be found when you least expect it.

As someone who is sensitive to the challenges and rewards associated with aging today, you undoubtedly have learned or will learn a great deal about yourself through this process. You most likely have made some decisions about how you want your aging process to evolve and what is important to you and your future. Unfortunately, we can't look into a crystal ball and see what our own aging journey will hold, but we can make plans for how we want to live as we age. Make those plans now and take steps to be the best senior you can be.

We have seen many families struggle with their senior care decisions. At times it is gut-wrenching and painful to watch. While it is one thing to make decisions for ourselves, it is quite another to make care decisions for someone we love. Emotions reign. Stress builds. And we are prone to second-guessing.

We pray that this book helps to inform you, motivate you, encourage you, and give you peace of mind that you are making the right choices for your loved one. Our hope is that this information will help rein in the emotions, reduce stress, and eliminate regret. Draw on God's strength. He is right there by your side saying, *Enjoy the journey, good and faithful servant!*

God bless you abundantly and give you peace.

Notes

Chapter 1

1. U.S. Department of Commerce, Bureau of the Census, "An Older and More Diverse Nation by Midcentury," press release, August 18, 2008, http://www.census.gov/Press-Release/www/releases/archives/population/012496.html (accessed February 16, 2009).

2. U.S. Department of Commerce, Bureau of the Census, "U.S. Population Projections, Table 5. Interim Projections. Population Under Age 18 and 65 and Older: 2000, 2010, and 2030," http://www.census.gov/population/www/projections/projectionsagesex.html (accessed February 16, 2009).

3. U.S. Department of Commerce, Bureau of the Census, "An Older and More Diverse Nation by Midcentury."

4. U.S. Department of Health and Human Services, Administration on Aging, *A Profile of Older Americans*, http://www.aoa.gov/AoAroot/Aging_Statistics/Profile/2003/2003profile.pdf (accessed February 16, 2009), 1.

5. U.S. Department of Commerce, Bureau of the Census, "Table 2a. Projected Population of the United States, by Age and Sex: 2000 to 2050," http://www.census.gov/population/www/projections/usinterimproj/natproj tab02a.pdf (Internet release date March 18, 2004; accessed February 16, 2009).

6. Office for National Statistics, United Kingdom. "Ageing: More pensioners than under-16's for first time ever," August 21, 2008, http://www.statistics.gov.uk/cci/nugget.asp?id=949 (accessed February 16, 2009).

7. U.S. Department of Commerce, Bureau of the Census, "Table 094: Midyear Population by Age and Sex," http://www.census.gov/ipc/www/idb/summaries.html (accessed March 11, 2009).

8. Australian Bureau of Statistics, *Population Projections, Australia, 2006 to 2101*, Cat. no. 3222.0, http://www.abs.gov.au/ausstats/abs@.nsf/ProductsbyCatalogue/5A9C0859C5F50C30CA25718C0015182F?OpenDocument (released September 2, 2008; accessed February 16, 2009).

9. World Health Organization, "Elderly people: Improving oral health amongst the elderly," http://www.who.int/oral_health/action/groups/en/index1 .html (accessed February 16, 2009).

10. National Association for Home Care and Hospice, "Basic Statistics About Home Care: Updated 2008," http://www.nahc.org/facts/08HC_Stats.pdf (accessed February 16, 2009).

11. U.S. Centers for Disease Control and Prevention, National Center for Health Statistics, "Health, United States, 2007. Table 117. Nursing homes, beds, occupancy, and residents, by geographic division and state: United States, selected years 1995–2006," http://www.cdc.gov/nchs/data/hus/ hus07.pdf#117 (accessed February 16, 2009), 387.

12. National Center for Assisted Living (NCAL), "Assisted Living Facility Profile," http://www.ncal.org/about/facility.cfm (accessed February 16, 2009). Excerpt provided courtesy of NCAL.

13. National Association for Home Care and Hospice, "Basic Statistics About Home Care: Updated 2008."

14. Memorandum from American Geriatrics Society to White House Conference on Aging Policy Committee, September 9, 2004, "Comments to the White House Conference on Aging Policy Committee," http://www .whcoa.gov/about/policy/meetings/summary/American_Geriatrics.pdf (accessed March 9, 2009).

15. National Academy of Elder Law Attorneys, "Media Fact Sheet," http:// www.naela.org/Media_FactSheet.aspx?Internal=true (accessed February 16, 2009). (National Academy of Elder Law Attorneys, 1577 Spring Hill Road, Suite 220, Vienna, VA 22182.)

16. U.S. Department of Commerce, Bureau of the Census, *The 65 Years and Over Population: 2000*, http://www.census.gov/prod/2001pubs/c2kbr01-10.pdf (issued October 2001; accessed February 16. 2009), 7.

17. U.S. Department of Commerce, Bureau of the Census, *Facts for Features*, "Older Americans Month: May 2008," http://www.census.gov/ Press-Release/www/releases/archives/cb08ff-06.pdf (issue date March 3, 2008; accessed February 16, 2009).

18. Ibid.

19. U.S. Department of Commerce, Bureau of the Census, "State and County QuickFacts, Washington, District of Columbia," http://quickfacts.census .gov/qfd/states/11/1150000.html (accessed February 16, 2009).

20. J. Lascaratos, G. Kalantzis, and E. Poulakou-Rebelakou, "Nursing Homes for the Old ('Gerocomeia') in Byzantium (324–1453 A.D.)," *Gerontology* 50, no. 2 (2004), http://content.karger.com/ProdukteDB/produkte .asp?Doi=75563 (accessed February 16, 2009), 113–17. Reproduced courtesy of S. Karger AG, Basel

21. The National Archives, United Kingdom, "Living in 1901: Old Age and the Workhouse," http://www.nationalarchives.gov.uk/pathways/census/living/health/work.htm (accessed February 19, 2008).

22. Ibid.

23. U.S. Social Security Administration, "Brief History: Otto von Bismarck, German Chancellor 1862–1890," http://www.ssa.gov/history/ottob.html (accessed February 16, 2009).

24. U.S. Social Security Administration, "Historical Background and Development of Social Security: Pre–Social Security Period," http://www.ssa.gov/history/briefhistory3.html (accessed March 11, 2009).

25. U.S. Department of Health and Human Services, Administration on Aging, *A Profile of Older Americans*, 2.

26. U.S. Department of Health and Human Services, Centers for Disease Control and Prevention, "Health Information for Older Adults," http://www.cdc.gov/aging/info.htm (accessed March 11, 2009).

27. Ibid.

28. Ibid.

29. AARP, *The State of 50 + America: 2006*, http://assets.aarp.org/rgcenter/econ/fifty_plus_2006.pdf (accessed February 16, 2009), 43.

30. Ibid., 46.

Chapter 2

1. Home Instead Senior Care, "40-70 Rule," http://www.4070talk.com. (accessed March 7, 2009).

2. Ibid.

3. Ibid.

4. Ibid.

5. Ibid.

6. Home Instead, Inc., *The 40-70 Rule: A Guide to Conversation Starters for Boomers and Their Senior Loved Ones*, 2008.

7. Ibid.

Chapter 3

1. U.S. National Institutes of Health, National Institute on Aging, *So Far Away: Twenty Questions for Long-Distance Caregivers*, "6. What is a geriatric care manager and how can I find one?" http://www.nia.nih.gov/HealthInformation/Publications/LongDistanceCaregiving/chapter06.htm (accessed March 10, 2009).

2. U.S. Department of Health and Human Services, Centers for Medicare and Medicaid Services, *Your Medicare Benefits*, http://www.medicare.gov/Publications/Pubs/pdf/10116.pdf (accessed on March 9, 2009), 13.

3. Ibid., 51.

4. U.S. National Institutes of Health, National Institute on Aging, *So Far Away: Twenty Questions for Long-Distance Caregivers*, http://www.nia.nih .gov/HealthInformation/Publications/LongDistanceCaregiving (March 9, 2009).
5. National Alliance for Caregiving, in collaboration with AARP, *Caregiving in the U.S.*, http://www.caregiving.org/data/04execsumm.pdf (accessed March 9, 2009), 8.
6. MetLife Mature Market Institute and National Alliance for Caregiving, *Miles Away: The MetLife Study of Long-Distance Caregiving*, http://www .caregiving.org/data/milesaway.pdf (accessed March 9, 2009), 2.
7. Ibid.
8. U.S. National Institutes of Health, National Institute on Aging, *So Far Away: Twenty Questions for Long-Distance Caregivers*, "1. What is Long-Distance Caregiving?" http://www.nia.nih.gov/HealthInformation/Publications/ LongDistanceCaregiving/chapter01.htm (accessed March 9, 2009).

Chapter 4

1. Seniorresource.com, "Ageing in Place," http://www.seniorresource.com/ ageinginpl.htm (accessed March 8, 2009).
2. Healthsense, "eNeighbor® System Components," http://www.healthsense .com/index.php/products/eneighbor-pers/eneighbor-system-components (accessed March 8, 2009).
3. Robots.net, "Toyota i-foot and i-unit Robot Vehicles," http://robots.net/ article/1356.html (accessed November 12, 2008).
4. Waseda University, "The successful robotic experiment made open to the public for the first time," http://www.waseda.jp/eng/news05/050429e.html (article dated April 25, 2005; accessed March 10, 2009).
5. Beacon Hill Village, "Lifestyle: Concierge and Services," http://www .beaconhillvillage.org/lifestyle.html (accessed March 8, 2009).
6. Naturally Occurring Retirement Community (NORCs)—An Aging in Place Initiative, http://www.norcs.com (accessed March 8, 2009).
7. Naturally Occurring Retirement Community (NORC) Blueprint—A Guide to Community Action, "Frequently Asked Questions," http://www .norcblueprint.org/faq (accessed March 8, 2009).
8. Naturally Occurring Retirement Community (NORC) Blueprint—A Guide to Community Action, "Lincoln Square Neighborhood Center, New York, NY," http://www.norcblueprint.org/stories/Lincoln_Square _Neighborhood_Center_NORC_program (accessed March 8, 2009).

Chapter 5

1. U.S. Department of Commerce, Bureau of the Census, "Census 2000 PHC-T-17. Multigenerational Households for the United States, States, and for Puerto Rico: 2000," http://www.census.gov/population/www/cen2000/briefs/phc-t17/tables/phc-t17.xls (accessed March 11, 2009).

2. Home Instead Senior Care, "How to Care for Yourself While Caring for Others," http://www.caregiverstress.com (accessed March 11, 2009).

3. National Family Caregivers Association and the National Alliance for Caregiving, "Caregiving Statistics," http://www.familycaregiving101.org/not_alone/stats.cfm (accessed March 11, 2009).

4. Evercare, in collaboration with the National Alliance for Caregiving, *Evercare Study of Family Caregivers—What They Spend, What They Sacrifice: The Personal Financial Toll of Caring for a Loved One*, http://www.caregiving.org/data/Evercare_NAC_CaregiverCostStudyFINAL20111907.pdf (accessed March 11, 2009), 7, 15.

5. Ibid.

6. Family Caregiver Alliance, "Home Away from Home: Relocating Your Parents," http://www.caregiver.org/caregiver/jsp/content_node.jsp?nodeid=849 (accessed March 11, 2009).

7. National Family Caregivers Association and the National Alliance for Caregiving, "Caregiving Statistics."

8. National Family Caregiver Association, "The Stress of Family Caregiving: Your Health May Be at Risk," *TAKE CARE! Self-Care for the Family Caregiver* (Winter 2006), http://www.thefamilycaregiver.org/pdfs/CaregiverStress.pdf (accessed March 11, 2009).

9. National Family Caregivers Association and National Alliance for Caregiving, "Caregiving Statistics."

10. Children of Aging Parents, "Caregiver Guide," http://www.caps4caregivers.org/guide.htm (accessed March 11, 2009).

11. National Family Caregivers Association and the National Alliance for Caregiving, "Caregiving Statistics."

Chapter 6

1. National Council on Aging, "Senior Center Fact Sheet," http://www.ncoa.org/content.cfm?sectionID=103&detail=2741 (accessed March 11, 2009).

2. Ibid.

3. National Adult Day Services Association, "Adult Day Services: Overview and Facts," http://www.nadsa.org/adsfacts/default.asp (accessed March 11, 2009).

4. U.S. Department of Health and Human Services, Administration on Aging, *Eldercare Locator*, "Adult Day Care Fact Sheet," http://www.eldercare.gov/

Eldercare.NET/Public/Resources/fact_sheets/adult_day.aspx (accessed March 11, 2009).

5. National Adult Day Services Association, "Adult Day Services: Overview and Facts."

6. U.S. Department of Health and Human Services, Administration on Aging, *Eldercare Locator*, "Adult Day Care Fact Sheet."

7. Helpguide.org, "Adult Day Care Centers: A Guide to Options and Selecting the Best Center for Your Needs," http://www.helpguide.org/elder/adult _day_care_centers.htm (accessed March 11, 2009).

8. U.S. Department of Commerce, Bureau of the Census, *Facts for Features*, "Women's History Month: March 2007," http://www.census.gov/ Press-Release/www/releases/archives/facts_for_features_special _editions/009383.html (press release dated January 4, 2007; accessed March 11, 2009).

9. Helpguide.org, "Adult Day Care Centers: A Guide to Options and Selecting the Best Center for Your Needs."

10. CareGuide@Home.com, "Adult Day Care: Peace of Mind While Out of the House," http://www.careguideathome.com/modules .php?op=modload&name=CG_Resources&file=article&sid=878 (accessed March 11, 2009).

11. Ibid.

12. Ibid.

13. National Adult Day Services Association, "Selecting Quality Providers," http://www.nadsa.org/quality_providers/default.asp (accessed March 11, 2009).

14. Ibid.

15. Ibid.

16. Family Caregiver Alliance (FCA), "Residential Care Options," http:// www.caregiver.org/caregiver/jsp/content_node.jsp?nodeid=1742 (accessed March 12, 2009).

Chapter 7

1. MetLife Mature Market Institute in conjunction with LifePlans, Inc., *The MetLife Market Survey of Adult Day Services & Home Care Costs* (September 2008), http://www.metlife.com/assets/cao/mmi/publications/studies/ mmi-studies-2008-adshc.pdf (accessed March 10, 2009), 4.

2. Ibid., 5.

3. Pan American Health Organization, "Women's Unremunerated Health Work," http://www.paho.org/English/ad/ge/UnremuneratedLabour.pdf (accessed March 10, 2009), 1. Reproduced with the permission of the Pan American Health Organization (PAHO). This fact sheet was originally published on PAHO's website: http://www.paho.org. To obtain information

about PAHO publications, visit their website at: http://publications.paho
.org.

4.   U.S. Department of Labor, Bureau of Labor Statistics, "Table 2, Fastest
     Growing Occupations, 2006–16," http://www.bls.gov/emp/emptab21.htm
     (accessed March 10, 2009).

Chapter 8

1.   U.S. Department of Health and Human Services, Centers for Medicare and
     Medicaid Services, *Home Health Prospective Payment System*, http://www.cms
     .hhs.gov/MLNProducts/downloads/HomeHlthProspPymtfctsht09-508.pdf
     (accessed March 9, 2009), 2.

Chapter 9

1.   CarePathways.com, "Independent Living Communities," http://www
     .carepathways.com/ILx.cfm (accessed March 10, 2009).
2.   Charles F. Longino, Jr., *Retirement Migration in America* (Houston, TX, Vaca-
     tion Publications, Inc., 2006).
3.   Ibid.
4.   Ibid.
5.   HelpGuide.org, "Continuing Care Retirement Communities," http://
     www.helpguide.org/elder/continuing_care_retirement_communities.htm
     (accessed December 21, 2008).

Chapter 10

1.   National Center for Assisted Living (NCAL), "Consumer Information,"
     http://www.ncal.org/consumer/index.cfm (accessed March 11, 2009).
     Excerpts provided courtesy of NCAL.
2.   Ibid.
3.   National Center for Assisted Living (NCAL), "Assisted Living Facility Pro-
     file." Excerpts provided courtesy of NCAL.
4.   Ibid.
5.   MetLife Mature Market Institute in conjunction with LifePlans, Inc., *The
     MetLife Market Survey of Nursing Home & Assisted Living Costs: October 2008*,
     http://www.metlife.com/assets/cao/mmi/publications/studies/
     mmi-studies-2008-nhal-costs.pdf (accessed March 11, 2009), 25.
6.   National Center for Assisted Living (NCAL). "Assisted Living Facility Pro-
     file." Excerpts provided courtesy of NCAL.
7.   Helpguide.org, "Assisted Living Facilities for Seniors," http://www
     .helpguide.org/elder/assisted_living_facilities.htm (accessed March 11,
     2009).

8. Center for Advancement of Health, "Strength Training May Help Elderly Rebuild Muscles, Improve Health," http://www.cfah.org/hbns/news/strength09-30-03.cfm (accessed March 11, 2009).

9. Ibid.

10. U.S. Centers for Disease Control and Prevention and the Alzheimer's Association, *The Healthy Brain Initiative: A National Public Health Road Map to Maintaining Cognitive Health* (2007), http://www.cdc.gov/aging/pdf/TheHealthyBrainInitiative.pdf (accessed March 9, 2009), 18.

11. Georgene Lahm, "Use It or Lose It Part 1: Brain Fitness," *Assisted Living Consult* 3, no. 6 (2007), http://www.assistedlivingconsult.com/issues/03-06/alc1112-Brain-1130.pdf (accessed March 11, 2009).

12. Dr. Michael Valenzuela, "Brain Reserve and Cognitive Decline: A Non-Parametric Systemic Review," *Psychological Medicine* 36, no. 8 (2006), quoted in Georgene Lahm, "Use It or Lose It Part 1: Brain Fitness," *Assisted Living Consult* 3, no. 6 (2007) http://www.assistedlivingconsult.com/issues/03-06/alc1112-Brain-1130.pdf (accessed March 11, 2009).

13. Georgene Lahm, "After Hours Activities in ALFs: Enhancing Resident Quality of Life," *Assisted Living Consult* 2, no. 2 (2006), http://www.assistedlivingconsult.com/issues/02-02/ALC02-02_AfterHours.pdf (accessed March 11, 2009).

14. Ibid.

15. Ibid.

16. Ibid.

17. Ibid.

Chapter 11

1. U.S. Centers for Disease Control and Prevention, National Center for Health Statistics, "Nursing Home Care," http://www.cdc.gov:80/nchs/fastats/nursingh.htm (accessed March 12, 2009).

2. Memorandum from Daniel R. Levinson, Inspector General, U.S. Department of Health and Human Services, to Kerry Weems, Centers for Medicare and Medicaid Services, September 18, 2008, "Trends in Nursing Home Deficiencies and Complaints," OEI-02-08-00140, http://www.oig.hhs.gov/oei/reports/oei-02-08-00140.pdf (accessed March 12, 2009).

3. MetLife Mature Market Institute in conjunction with LifePlans, Inc., *The MetLife Market Survey of Nursing Home & Assisted Living Costs: October 2008.*

4. U.S. Department of Health and Human Services, Centers for Medicare and Medicaid Services, *Medicare Coverage of Skilled Nursing Facility Care*, http://www.medicare.gov/publications/pubs/pdf/10153.pdf (accessed March 11, 2009), 3.

5. Ibid., 13.

Chapter 12

1. National Hospice and Palliative Care Organization, "What Is Hospice and Palliative Care?" http://www.nhpco.org/i4a/pages/index.fm?pageid=4648 (accessed December 30, 2008).

2. U.S. Department of Health and Human Services, Centers for Medicare and Medicaid Services, *Payment System Fact Sheet Series: Hospice Payment System*, http://www.cms.hhs.gov/MLNProducts/downloads/hospice_pay_sys_fs .pdf (accessed March 11, 2009), 2.

3. National Hospice and Palliative Care Organization from the Caring Connections website, "Begin Hospice Care," http://www.caringinfo.org/LivingWithAnIllness/Hospice/BeginHospiceCare.htm (accessed December 30, 2008).

4. U.S. Department of Health and Human Services, Centers for Medicare and Medicaid Services, *Payment System Fact Sheet Series: Hospice Payment System*, 3.

5. National Hospice and Palliative Care Organization, "History of Hospice Care," http://www.nhpco.org/i4a/pages/index.cfm?pageid=3285 (accessed March 11, 2009).

6. National Hospice and Palliative Care Organization from the Caring Connections website, "Paying for Hospice," http://www.caringinfo.org/Living WithAnIllness/Hospice/PayingForHospice.htm (accessed December 30, 2008).

7. U.S. Department of Health and Human Services, Centers for Medicare and Medicaid Services, *Medicare Hospice Data 1998–2005*, http://www.cms.hhs .gov/ProspMedicareFeeSvcPmtGen/downloads/HospiceData1998-2005.pdf (accessed March 11, 2009), 2.

8. U.S. Department of Health and Human Services, Administration on Aging, *Preparing to Say Good-Bye: Care for the Dying*, http://www.aoa.gov/prof/aoaprog/caregiver/carefam/taking_care_of_others/docs/echo3.pdf (accessed March 12, 2009), 4.

9. U.S. Department of Health and Human Services, Administration on Aging, *A Hospice Care Guide for Families*, http://www.docstoc.com/docs/3470060/U-S-Department-of-Health-and-Human-Services-Administration-on (accessed May 26, 2009), 1.

10. National Hospice and Palliative Care Organization, "What Is Hospice and Palliative Care?"

11. National Hospice and Palliative Care Organization, "Hospice Care Saves Money for Medicare, New Study Shows," http://www.nhpco.org/i4a/pages/Index.cfm?pageID=5386 (accessed December 30, 2008).

12. U.S. Department of Health and Human Services, Centers for Medicare and Medicaid Services, *Payment System Fact Sheet Series: Hospice Payment System*, 2.

13. Ibid., 3.

14. Ibid.

15. National Hospice and Palliative Care Organization from the Caring Connections website, "Begin Hospice Care."

16. U.S. Department of Health and Human Services, Administration on Aging, "Alzheimer's Disease Demonstration Grants to States: Volunteer Respite Programs," www.aoa.gov/AoARoot/AoA_Programs/HCLTC/Alz _Grants/docs/VolunteerRespitePrograms.doc (accessed May 26, 2009).

17. U.S. Department of Health and Human Services, Centers for Medicare and Medicaid Services, *Medicare Hospice Benefits*, http://www.medicare.gov/ publications/Pubs/pdf/02154.pdf (accessed March 12, 2009), 6.

Chapter 13

1. U.S. Federal Trade Commission, *Funerals: A Consumer Guide*, http://www .ftc.gov/bcp/edu/pubs/consumer/products/pro19.shtm (accessed March 9, 2009).

2. Homefuneral.com, "A Home Funeral Is Green, and It's Legal," http:// homefuneral.info (accessed March 9, 2009).

3. Funeral Consumers Alliance, Inc. "Four-Step Funeral Planning," http:// www.funerals.org/frequently-asked-questions/general/141-four-step -funeral-planning (accessed March 9, 2009).

4. Homefuneral.com. "A Home Funeral Is Green, and It's Legal."

5. U.S. Department of Health and Human Services, Administration on Aging, *When Death Occurs: What to Do When a Loved One Dies*, http://www.aoa .gov/prof/aoaprog/caregiver/carefam/taking_care_of_others/docs/ ECHO4.pdf (accessed March 10, 2009), 7.

6. Funeralplan.com, "How to Plan a Funeral," http://www.funeralplan.com/ funeralplan/about/how.html (accessed January 9, 2009).

7. U.S. Federal Trade Commission, *Facts for Consumers*, "Paying Final Respects: Your Rights When Buying Funeral Goods & Services," http://www.ftc .gov/bcp/edu/pubs/consumer/products/pro26.pdf (accessed March 9, 2009).

8. Ibid.

9. U.S. National Institutes of Health, National Institute on Aging, "Things to Do After Someone Dies," http://www.nia.nih.gov/HealthInformation/ Publications/endoflife/06_things.htm.htm (accessed March 10, 2009).

10. Ibid.

11. Ibid.

12. U.S. Federal Trade Commission, *Funerals: A Consumer Guide*.

13. Ibid.

14. Ibid.

15. Ibid.

16. Ibid.

17. National Caregivers Library, "Funeral Costs," http://www.caregiverslibrary .org/Default.aspx?tabid=356 (accessed March 9, 2009). (Source: www .CaregiversLibrary.org. The National Caregivers Library is an extensive online library focused on the needs of caregivers, their families, and the organizations that serve or employ them. Article reprinted with permission from FamilyCare America, Inc., Richmond, Virginia.)

Chapter 14

1. Athealth.com, "Bereavement and Grief," http://www.athealth.com/ Consumer/Disorders/Bereavement.html (accessed March 8, 2009).
2. Chaplaincy Services and Pastoral Education, University of Virginia Health System, "What Do I Do Now?" http://www.healthsystem.virginia.edu/ internet/chaplaincy/bereavement/what.cfm (accessed March 8, 2009).
3. Athealth.com, "Bereavement and Grief."
4. Ibid.
5. U.S. Department of Health and Human Services, Administration on Aging, National Family Caregiver Support Program, *Help for the Bereaved, The Healing Journey*, http://www.aoa.gov/prof/aoaprog/caregiver/carefam/taking _care_of_others/docs/ECHO5.pdf (accessed March 9, 2009).
6. Athealth.com, "Bereavement and Grief."

Chapter 15

1. U.S. Department of Health and Human Services, Substance Abuse and Mental Health Services Administration, *Co-Occurring Disorder-Related Quick Facts: Elderly*, http://www.coce.samhsa.gov/cod_resources/PDF/Elderly QuickFacts.pdf (accessed March 10, 2009).
2. U.S. Centers for Disease Control and Prevention and National Association of Chronic Disease Directors, "The State of Mental Health and Aging in America Issue Brief 1: What Do the Data Tell Us?" http://www.cdc.gov/ aging/pdf/mental_health.pdf (accessed March 10, 2009).
3. U.S. Department of Health and Human Services, Centers for Disease Control and Prevention, "Alzheimer's Disease," http://www.cdc.gov/aging/ healthybrain/alzheimers.htm (accessed March 10, 2009).
4. U.S. Department of Health and Human Services, Administration on Aging, "Alzheimer's Disease Information: AoA Fact Sheet on Alzheimer's Disease," http://www.aoa.gov/AoARoot/Press_Room/Products_Materials/pdf/ fs_Alzheimer.doc (accessed May 26, 2009).
5. AgingCare.com—The Community for Caregivers of Aging Parents, "Health Conditions: Alzheimer's & Dementia," http://www.agingcare.com/Health -Conditions/1133/Alzheimer-s-Dementia (accessed March 10, 2009).
6. Ibid.

7. U.S. National Institutes of Health, National Institute on Aging, "Alzheimer's Disease Medications Fact Sheet," http://www.nia.nih.gov/Alzheimers/ Publications/medicationsfs.htm (accessed March 10, 2009).
8. U.S. Department of Health and Human Services, Centers for Disease Control and Prevention, "Falls Among Older Adults: An Overview," http:// www.cdc.gov/ncipc/factsheets/adultfalls.htm (accessed March 10, 2009).
9. AgingCare.com—The Community for Caregivers of Aging Parents, "Health Conditions: Parkinson's Disease," http://www.agingcare.com/Health-Conditions/1140/Parkinson-s-Disease (accessed March 10, 2009).
10. AgingCare.com—The Community for Caregivers of Aging Parents, "Dealing with the Daily Challenges of Parkinson's Disease," http://www .agingcare.com/Featured-Stories/119724/Dealing-with-the-Daily -Challenges-of-Parkinson-s-Disease.htm (accessed March 10, 2009).
11. U.S. Centers for Disease Control and Prevention with Merck Company Foundation, *The State of Aging and Health in America 2007*, http://www.cdc .gov/aging/pdf/saha_2007.pdf (accessed March 10, 2009), 13.
12. Ibid., 6.
13. AgingCare.com—The Community for Caregivers of Aging Parents, "Health Conditions: Diabetes," http://www.agingcare.com/Health-Conditions/ 1134/Diabetes (accessed March 10, 2009).
14. AgingCare.com—The Community for Caregivers of Aging Parents, "Caring for a Diabetic," http://www.agingcare.com/Featured-Stories/117356/ Caring-for-a-Diabetic.htm (accessed March 10, 2009).

Chapter 16
1. U.S. Department of Health and Human Services, Administration on Aging, *Chapter 4: Dealing with Challenging Behaviors*, http://www.aoa.gov/alz/ media/pdf/housing/Chapter4.pdf (accessed March 11, 2009).
2. Ibid.
3. U.S. Department of Health and Human Services, Administration on Aging, "Because We Care—What Housing Options Are Available?" http://www .aoa.gov/prof/aoaprog/caregiver/carefam/taking_care_of_others/wecare/ housing-options.aspx (accessed March 11, 2009).
4. Michigan Long-Term Care Ombudsman, *Guardianship and Nursing Home Residency: What Rights Does an Individual Retain?* http://www.michigan.gov/ documents/miseniors/GuardianshipNHResidency_194206_7.pdf (accessed March 11, 2009).
5. Ibid.
6. Family Caregiver Alliance, "Holding a Family Meeting," http://www.care giver.org/caregiver/jsp/content_node.jsp?nodeid=475 (accessed February 5, 2009).

7. Connie Matthiessen, Caring.com, "Caring for Your Elderly Parents: How to Handle Family Conflicts," http://www.caring.com/articles/family-conflicts-and-sibling-rivalry-caring-for-elderly-parents (accessed February 5, 2009).

8. Connie Matthiessen, Caring.com, "Caring for Your Difficult Parent," http://www.caring.com/articles/caring-for-your-difficult-parent (accessed February 5, 2009).

9. Ibid.

Chapter 17

1. MetLife Mature Market Institute in conjunction with LifePlans, Inc., *The MetLife Market Survey of Nursing Home & Assisted Living Costs: October 2008.*

2. Patricia Barry, "Silver Surge: Who Will Take Care of Aging Boomers?" *AARP Bulletin Today* (May 9, 2008), http://bulletin.aarp.org/yourhealth/caregiving/articles/silver_surge__who.html (accessed March 10, 2009).

3. U.S. Department of Housing and Urban Development, "Top Ten Things to Know if You're Interested in a Reverse Mortgage," http://www.hud.gov/offices/hsg/sfh/hecm/rmtopten.cfm (accessed March 10, 2009).

4. U.S. Department of Health and Human Services, Centers for Medicare and Medicaid Services, "Long-Term Care," http://www.medicare.gov/LongTermCare/Static/Home.asp (accessed March 10, 2009).

5. Helpguide.org, "Payment Options for Senior Housing and Residential Care," http://www.helpguide.org/elder/paying_for_senior_housing_residential_care.htm (accessed March 10, 2009).

6. AARP, *Myths About the Medicaid Program and The People It Helps*, http://www.aarp.org/research/assistance/medicaid/fs116_myths.html#FOOT1 (accessed Jan. 27, 2009).

Chapter 18

1. Rosalynn Carter, "Addressing the Caregiving Crisis," *Preventing Chronic Disease* 5, no. 2 (2008), http://www.cdc.gov/pcd/issues/2008/jan/07_0162.htm (accessed March 8, 2009).

2. U.S. Department of Health and Human Services: *Womenshealth.gov*, "Frequently Asked Questions: Caregiver Stress," http://www.womenshealth.gov/faq/caregiver-stress.cfm (accessed March 8, 2009).

3. Family Caregiver Alliance, "Taking Care of YOU: Self-Care for Family Caregivers," http://www.caregiver.org/caregiver/jsp/content_node.jsp?nodeid=847 (accessed March 11, 2009).

4. U.S. Department of Health and Human Services: *Womenshealth.gov*, "Frequently Asked Questions: Caregiver Stress," http://www.womenshealth.gov/faq/caregiver-stress.cfm (accessed March 8, 2009).

5. Ibid.

Chapter 19

1. U.S. Centers for Disease Control and Prevention's National Center for Health Statistics, *Health, United States, 2007*, http://www.cdc.gov/nchs/data/hus/hus07.pdf#027 (accessed Feb. 19, 2009), 192.

2. U.S. Department of Health and Human Services, Centers for Disease Control and Prevention, "Obesity, High Blood Pressure Impacting Many U.S. Adults Ages 55–64," http://www.cdc.gov/od/oc/media/pressrel/r051208.htm (accessed Feb. 19, 2009).

3. U.S. Department of Health and Human Services, Centers for Disease Control and Prevention, "Number of People with Diabetes Increases to 24 Million," http://www.cdc.gov/media/pressrel/2008/r080624.htm?s_cid=mediarel_r080624_x (accessed Feb. 19, 2009).

4. H. Chen and X. Guo, "Obesity and functional disability in elderly Americans," *Journals of the American Geriatrics Society* 56, no. 4 (2008), quoted in Robin Arnette, "Indicators of Obesity are Related to Disability in the Elderly," *Environmental Factor* (June 2008), a publication of the U.S. National Institute of Environmental Health Sciences, http://www.niehs.nih.gov/news/newsletter/2008/june/intramuralpapers.cfm (accessed March 7, 2009).

5. U.S. Department of Health and Human Services, Centers for Disease Control and Prevention, "Alzheimer's Disease."

6. U.S. Department of Health and Human Services, Administration on Aging's National Family Caregiver Support Program, *Advance Care Planning: Making Choices Known* (2002, 2004), http://www.aoa.gov/prof/aoaprog/caregiver/carefam/taking_care_of_others/docs/ECHO1.pdf (accessed March 7, 2009), 8.

7. Ibid., 12.

8. Ibid, 6.

9. Ibid., 18.

10. U.S. Department of Health and Human Services, Centers for Medicare and Medicaid Services, "National Health Expenditures, 2007 Highlights," http://www.cms.hhs.gov/NationalHealthExpendData/downloads/highlights.pdf (accessed Feb. 19, 2009), 2.

11. Ibid.

12. U.S. Department of Health and Human Services, Centers for Medicare and Medicaid Services, "Medicaid Spending Projected to Rise Much Faster than the Economy," http://www.cms.hhs.gov/apps/media/press/release.asp?Counter=3311&intNumPerPage=10&checkDate=&checkKey=&srchType=1&numDays=350 (news release dated October 17, 2008; accessed March 7, 2009).

Index